REFLECTION OF THE SHADOW DANCER

BEVERLY L. ANDERSON

Phoenix Voices Publishing

Contents

This is dedicated to my friends that I have made in the shadows of the world. This is for the ones who don't conform to the standard, and are different and unique in some way.

Without the dark, there can be no light. Without the light, there can be no dark. And in between, lies the shadow.

PROLOGUE

THE SHADOW DANCER'S MIRROR

The mirror stands floor to ceiling in this tiny studio. No one else looks into the depths of this reflective surface except for one single dancer. For a second, the figure stands and is utterly still in the room. Then, she lifts her hands up above her head and begins to dance. She moves like molten silver in the utter silence and emptiness of this once boisterous and vibrant place. The echoes of this place

Dust has piled high along the opposite wall, filling the cracks and crevices of rows and rows of trophies shelved there. Tiny golden ballerinas and perfect little tap dancers grace the tops of ivory, marble, and quartz columns. Numbers one through ten can be seen on various statues on the solid oak shelves. Names are etched in some, but none can be read anymore. Some are coated with tarnish where the silver parts have aged, and others have rusted where moisture settled on some metal part of the trophy.

The silence would be deafening, if any, but the dancer was in graffiti graces the old boards, layers and layers over the years. The street itself has become a lonely and terrible place, smelling of human refuse and filth. The buildings around the tiny studio have long been homes to animals and homeless people, most of which are unhealthy either in body or mind. No more than ten miles away, a grand theater puts on a world-renowned ballet tonight. When the wind is right, the somber tones of the music can be heard here.

The glass of the window, choked with dust and cobwebs, somehow has remained unbroken. The small studio has somehow remained unmolested by thieves, vandals, and miscreants. The oak door is no stronger than the neighbor's door. The glass is not unbreakable, but it stands still despite being the largest glass window on the street. Eventually, it was boarded up not because of being broken like so many of the other windows but because it was not broken.

The rhythm of her dance is unbroken, and she is unbothered by any of these things. Up on toes, down on heels, spinning left, spinning right, leaping skyward, she dances on and on. She is safe here. No one can enter this place while she dances here. No one can harm her here. No, she dances here day and night, and no one sees, no one hears, but she dances on.

Dawn breaks, and through the boards on the great front window, dusty dawn sunshine filters into the once colorfully painted room. The walls were once brilliant pink with murals of dancers in various poses in every color of the rainbow. Those images are faded now; these smudged remnants of the happy dancers are all that remain. The pink is so faded and stained with time it has become a sick yellow and salmon color. The wooden bar in front of the dancer's mirror is splintered and fractured, rotted through in places, with the rusty brackets starting to pull away from the wood in places.

Yet she dances on. Unreal and real at the same time, she is here and isn't here. Was she once alive? Is she dead now? Is she a ghost? Is she a protector of this place she once loved so dearly?

She is but a shadow, a shadow dancer, in this world now.

She pauses and contemplates the light filtering in through the window into her hands and through her hands. In the mirror, the light reflects, and she stares into it, quiet and still for now.

ACT I

DANCES OF LIGHT

Soft light filters into her and through her at the same time. Soft, subtle, but so brilliant at the same time. She begins to dance once more, no more frozen in place by the entrance of the morning's light. Outside, birds begin their morning ritual of singing sweetly to each other, but inside the studio, that sound is muffled by the music that no one can hear. The Shadow Dancer swirls around the room, hearing something that is beyond anything in this world, and moving her body with grace that only she can see in her own reflection.

Uplifting music reverberates silently, with large crescendos and bright and brilliant sounds. Bells, trumpets, flutes, and rich beautiful sounds that brighten the soul and tell stories with no words fill the room. Sounds of love and hope bring a spring to her step that nothing else can. The world is pale compared to the music's grandiose and glorious sound.

Stories of love, both lost and won, seem to fill the souls of those who are not there to listen. Overcoming pain, hurt and becoming one with the world once again are lofty goals reached

She dances with grace and leaps across the room, and outside the world moves on. The soup kitchen two doors down opens its doors for breakfast, filling quickly with the homeless of this once bustling street. A man of twenty-five years who spent five of the last six overseas watching his friends die helps a little girl who lost her father six months ago to cancer. Her mom desperately clutches her eight-month-old son to her chest and weeps as she takes the handed-out food, toast and butter. The young veteran comforts her, even though he is at least five years younger than her.

The day moves on, and the Shadow Dancer continues her dance. The people move on, and despite having nothing, they leave the warmth of the soup kitchen with a spark of hope in their hearts for it is a new day. Around the corner, a job may be waiting. A friend that wants to give them a hand may walk up to them and take them out of this life. With the sun, new hope is brought.

Touch the Stars

Such is my way to the
stars,
tightly   bound   with
chains and bars.

As it will be, it will be.
Always and truly, forev-
er.
They bind me, do you
not see?
But my spirit will die
never.

My spirit they hurt, try
to break,
but my spirit will not be
broken.
A martyr of me, they
will make
if here and now I die un-
broken.

Such is my way to the
stars,
tightly   bound   with
chains and bars.

Soon I will die a grisly
death
in front of all those who
love me

but that is what they
need, my death.
to open their eyes, let
them see.

How cruel and unjust
the oppressors are,
I   did   nothing   but
chanced to speak,
and they dragged me
out, old and weak,
I smile a good smile; I
will touch the stars.

The Breath of Life

Have you ever listened?
I mean, really listened?
And heard?
I have.
And what I have heard
is my soul breathing
life.
Silent.
And I am sitting.
Listening to quiet.
Listening to empti-
ness.
Listening to nothing.
And hearing every-
thing
in the universe.
Silently as I sit,
hearing the sound,
the wonderful sound,
and I am alone.
I have heard my soul
breathe,
and now I am truly alive.

Destiny's Touch

The cosmos spin as
they have for time un-
known.
And down here people
are born and later they
die.

Diamonds   sprinkled
liberally against
a thick curtain of black
velvet.
And there was mapped
out the destiny of a
child.

A hot afternoon, late
July, the sign of fire,
the sign of the lion,
ruled by double suns.

I arrived two weeks ear-
ly,
no doubt in a hurry
to meet the world out-
side,
and glad that my mom
gambled with her life
rather than rid herself of
me.
The doctor, mom and
me were only present,

and we all made it out of
the delivery room.
At least that's what she
told me.
I'm not sure anymore if
that's true.

Purple became my col-
or.
The color of royalty, the
color of spiritual pow-
er.

In China, I am a Mon-
key for the year 1980.
My father was gone,
mom said he didn't care,
and he left us.
I have a step father that
would become my dad
for life.

South Texas Summers
never tanned my skin
and I envied the Latina
girls for their color.
Too much English and
German blood in me, as
I am still
pale and freckled in the
sun.

Grandma died when I
was young.
It made me sad but I

understood that people
died.
A few years later it was
grandpa that left us
and it was true that peo-
ple don't live for a long
time.
I thought that every
time a person died
a new star was born.

I don't think I believe
that any more.

My best friend was
Kim,
and we spent a lot of
time with each other,
and it was because
sometimes we were all
we had.
Julie was another friend,
and then there were
three of us.

I played a flute in band.
I wasn't very good, but
we had fun.

The Celtic stars have
branded me a unicorn.
I collect figures and pic-
tures of unicorns.
I have a great many from
the years.

I was never going to
leave. I was home.
I had a no good father, a
worthless sister
and only mom cared.

But still I cried.

I made friends with my
sister though
and found that my
mom's words were not
all that true.

Across the miles of laid
phone lines,
I made friends who did
not judge me.
I wanted to be new.
I wanted to be my own
person,
and that was how I be-
came
the Phoenix.
Reborn with what I
wished to be.

At school I majored in
Psychology
since I was good at lis-
tening to people.
I didn't really want to be
that,
because all I wanted to

do was write.
But writers don't make
much money,
so I found something
that would.

The Time of Arthur has
said that I am
the Red Dragon of
Arthur and
the Oak tree is sacred to
me.
That is nice too, because
I have many dragons as
well,
and the oak tree is my fa-
vorite tree.
We had many of them at
home.
Another sign of fire.

The   phone   lines
brought me more than
friendship,
though it was not some-
thing that I was seek-
ing.
Mike was in Missouri
and he seemed like a nice
guy.
Soon my heart fluttered
to see him come on-
line.

Destiny's touch brushed

my cheek.

The computer crashed,
and we resorted to the
phone.
We talked a lot and of-
ten.
He came to meet me
and we felt we were truly
soul-mated.
I cried when he flew
home, and so did he.

Missouri welcomed me
with a terrible snowy
winter.
I'd never seen snow be-
fore.
Things were different
here and I found I could
do
anything for the one I
loved.

Back home they
thought that I was not
doing the right
thing by leaving every-
one,
and Mom did not let me
forget.

I called home for
Christmas and she said
that

she'd lost the house.
My heart hurt but there
was nothing for me to
do.

Then they found the
monster that was eating
her from inside out.
They thought that it was
gone after I was born
but now it sat
like a foul beast inside
her stomach.

She died near Mother's
Day, and I remember
feeling
such pain at seeing the
"Remember Mom"
signs at my work,
JCPenney.

I felt pain at not being
there, but at least my sis-
ter made
amends with her after all
those years.

I grew used to this
place,
though there was much
that was not to my lik-
ing.
Too many people that
were all the same.

But there was nothing
to be done.

I had a family, though it
was not my own.
I married my best friend
on December 1, 2001.

I wish mom had been
there to see it,
because she'd said she
was sad that she couldn't
see my children.
At least in death she's
found peace.
She never knew it in
life.

I found friends up here
too, though I missed
those down there.
That is still home.

Brenda is a name that
comes from Brandr,
which is an old Norse
word meaning sword.
My name means Fiery
Sword in most interpre-
tations,
and sometimes just
fire.
I collect swords as
well, and other bladed
weapons.

Good friends kept my
mind well,
and we played games,
and we had fun.
I met a person that I
swore was my twin, in
mind and soul
and it's interesting.
She showed me the way
to something I thought
of but never did.
But in the end I was be-
trayed, and I found out
sometimes
people are in our lives
for a reason or lesson.
Since then, hearts have
mended, and my friend
is more than that now.

School has taught me
what I believe.
It's not by what it has
said but what I have be-
come by being here.
It's not really learning
but discovering myself.

A game has become a
part of my life.
Like writing with
friends.

And the spirit still

leads me to interesting
places.

My father is not what
my mother had said.
A sweet man who is sor-
ry he wasn't there,
but it was mom that
chased him away.
I believe what he says for
mom was not the nicest
person always.
I love him and only just
met him.
He and I are alike in
many ways and the psy-
chologist in me says
that that cannot be, per-
sonality isn't that genet-
ic.

I'm rethinking that idea,
though.

Soon enough life turned
and my son was born
though he took thirty
hours and had his hand
upon his head.

A psychologist I'd never
be, I returned to school
to teach this time lan-
guage and poetry to kids
one day soon.

Maybe one of them
would love it as much as
I do.
But when life took me
away, I found a new call-
ing,
as new life grew within
me.

Not to teach, I was
called to help as a coun-
selor,
though not in the way I
thought I would.
This time, he came
in three hours, cord
around his neck,
and again my world
changed.

Now, returned where I
once began my jour-
ney,
I'm discovering parts of
myself that I never knew
about.
It seems I am not as sim-
ple as I once believed.

Destiny's Touch has al-
ways been there,
written across the stars.

Otherwise there is no
way to explain my life.

Dying Fire

The fire drips from my
fingers
in burning crimson
flames.
My mouth is all afire
and all is lost.
Flaming torches burn
my flesh
as swords pierce my
heart,
swords of tempered
fire.
Burning fluid heat,
burning inside out.
A gasping fire burns in
the pit of my soul
and I am surely dying,
as the fire of my very be-
ing flows forth
To set the whole world
afire.

The Night Wind

The night wind blows
my fears away.
As I sit outside in the
darkness.
My fear is of the things
in this world.
I fear life.
I fear death.

And all the things in be-
tween the two.
It brings me into the
dark,
this fear.

I ponder my life as I
let the night wind cool
me.
I wish I knew why we are
here.
I know not why as I sit in
the night wind.

It breezes in my mind,
Helping me to find lost
answers
that I want to know.

I know this fear will
never go away.
I can only wait for an

answer
in the night wind.

I know you can avoid
this fear,
but only for a little
while.
I face this fear with eyes
open wide,
Ready for anything I
must face.

Fear is everywhere you
look.
You can face it or run
away.
If you run, you must
face it anyway.
If you turn and face it,
you can make it easier.
Try this sometime.

Just sit outside in the
cool night wind.
Things will get clearer.
Let the wind run
through your mind,
and you will see.

You will find those lost
answers
that are in your mind
With the help of the
night wind.

I Will Follow Thee

Deep into the depths of
hell,
I will follow thee.
Till I hear the tolling
bell,
I will follow thee.

I carry in my very soul,
a little piece of your
heart,
so that I may find you,
should you and I ever
part.

Take me into your silent
arms,
One final time and all is
fine.
And before I go, you
must know,
Always I'm yours and
you are mine.

Now, I slip away into the
dark,
Will you follow me?
I know in your heart I
made my mark,
Will you follow me?

The Place of My Desire

Into the rich, red flames
I desire,
I descend into mine own
fire.
Poeticus furor, please
consume me,
Take me far away and
please let me see.
While all within me does
burn,
Oh, from the flames, let
me learn.
Take away from my
heart the chain,
Take away from my soul
the pain.
Fire from my hand doth
pour.
Like blood from an
open sore.
The fire, it will consume
me, all,
But it will uphold me,
I'll not fall.
It will take me down, in
truth, all.
The blood is gushing
too fast from the sore.
The fire still comes, for-
ever to pour.

In my soul there is a
fresh pain,
In my heart there is a
new chain.
The flame is too hot, no
more to learn
Except how it feels for
me to burn.
I have, in truth, seen all
there is to see,
The poetical fire has
consumed me.
No sadness, I am deep in
my fire,
This is the lonely place
of my desire.

Around and Through

Seeing around,
through the dark,
through the light,
and I know.

The Protector's Question

To protect me you are
sworn.
But when I arrive, will
you?
I'm yours just as I am
born,
So small and so very
new.
Before I can come to
light
I must ask you one
question.
Then I shall come from
my night,
Can I count on protec-
tion?
Will you always be there
to take care of me?
Will you love me like no
other?
Will you help me learn
and be?
Will you stay and be my
mother?
Or will you kill me deep
inside?
Will you hurt the seed
you have sown?
Will you let me say you
have lied?

And will you leave me all
alone?
I don't know what waits
out there.
I hope you love me, dear
heart,
Because I need you to
care.
Please bring me out of
the dark.
I must trust you with my
life,
Hold out your hands as
I fall.
Catch me, take me into
strife.
Just hold me with love,
that's all.

On Fantasy

The truth in life
is what you can touch.
Anything else
is mere fantasy.
Or so they say.
What is impossible
is not real,
or is it?
What if it is not impos-
sible,
merely improbable?
Would that change
our thoughts
on the real and imagi-
nary?
Would it change
Anything?

Sing Sweet Lullaby

Sing sweet lullaby,
So, please, don't you
cry.
Lay your head down to
rest.
I will stand to the test.
I'll keep away the
night.
I'll scare away your
fright.
I won't let harm come to
you,
because I know what to
do.
So sleep upon your pil-
low,
And I'll sing so sweet
and low.
Slip all your so quiet
reams
Where you know every-
thing means.
Slip into your silent
sleep.
I'll see that those dreams
you'll keep.
So, please don't you
cry,
Sing sweet lullaby.

Your Angel

I'll be your angel, baby.
I'll come and lift you
up.
I'll be your angel, baby.
I'll take you high
enough.

When I came down to
you,
you were so low you
didn't even see
that you needed to open
your heart,
so I handed you that
very key.

Look into my eyes, baby,
look deep.
You will see the love that
waits there.
You will see just how
much you mean
and how much I truly
care.

I'll be your angel, baby.
I'll come and lift you
up.
I'll be your angel, baby.
I'll take you high
enough.

So come to me sweetly,
my darling',
I'll hold you when you
cry.
Give it all away to me,
baby.
Kiss it all good-bye...

I'll wrap you up in my
love,
and I'll hold you oh so
tight,
I'll kiss away all those
tears,
and I'll be your very
light.

I'll be your angel, baby.
I'll come and lift you
up.
I'll be your angel, baby.
I'll take you high
enough.

I'm gonna hold you in
my arms,
all through the dark
night.
Then I'm gonna love
away your fears,
still holding you oh so
tight.

You're never gonna be

afraid.
You're never gonna hurt
again.
for that is why I was
sent.
and how I've taken away
the chain.

That   heavy   chain
around your heart,
I pulled it away so you
could be free,
for it has been holding
you back,
and now in light you can
see...

I'll be your angel, baby.
I'll come and lift you
up.
I'll be your angel, baby.
I'll   take   you   high
enough.

Yeah, I'll be your angel,
I'll wrap you in my lov-
ing embrace.
I'll give you love and
forgiveness,
as I look into your open
face.

I'll be your angel, baby.
I'll come and lift you
up.

I'll be your angel, baby.
I'll take you high
enough.

I'm your angel baby,
your saving grace.
I'm your angel baby...
Always your angel.

Reaching Out

Her eyes are pleading
with me
As she looks up from the
dark.
Do I help her?
I am in the light.
I reach down into the
dark.
It doesn't hurt me.
It is much easier to slip
into the dark
than to climb into the
light.
She's reaching up as far
as she can,
but it burns her.
I grip her hand and pull
her up.
I pull her slowly from
the abyss.
She's in pain, but I'm
here.
I won't let her slip back
in.
Not now that I have
pulled her out.
And she's holding to me
for dear life.
She's out, but it is hard
to stay out.
She lets go and hangs

onto my hand.
It is enough, she's in the
light.
And she'll stay here
for as long as she wants.

Hold!

Hold!
Don't drop what you
have.
What is it that you
have?
Do you even know?
You don't know
how precious and frag-
ile,
how glass and crystal,
how delicate and secret
what you hold is.
Do you even know?

Hold!
Don't let it slip
and shatter like
the champagne glass
thrown into the fire-
place
after the kiss.

Hold!
Keep it near.
Don't let go of
my heart.

Truth to Face the Other

Seeking the truth
will bring you things
you do not want to see.
It will make you see
inside your soul.
See things that
you do not want to see.
In the soul exists
possibility.
Possibility of what you
are.
In each exists
the possibility to be-
come
angel or devil.
You must face the oth-
er
when you seek the truth.

Letter to Love

Dear Love,
Here you are now down
deep inside.
You have laid this heart
open wide.
Something I've never
thought or known
The way to the light you
have shown.
You have set my head to
spin,
And my soul to stir
within.
No one had been able to
reach me
With a heart closed, yet
you could see.
I did not want it, no, not
before,
Now I have held it, and I
want more.
So, love, now to me you
came
And nothing will be the
same.
My heart beats steady
and true
And all I ever want is
you.
Love, Me.

Fire and Ice

The nerves in my body
burn to the tone of fire,
like all or nothing.
The nerves in my body
freeze to the tone of
ice,
like all or nothing.
Hot pain rushes,
to be relieved by the
cold.
Cold pain rushes,
to be relieved by the
heat.
Fire that burns
extinguished by ice that
cools.
Ice that freezes
melted by fire that
warms.
Phoenix of fire?
Phoenix or ice?
One in the same.
Freezing heat,
Searing cold.
Each destroying me
completely
to be reborn into the
other
at the same moment.
Will I survive to be re-
born?

Wedding Vow

We are all born split in
twain,
We are all born half of a
whole.
In life we seek the oth-
er,
The rest of our very
soul.
Soul mates we have al-
ways been.
Soul mates we shall al-
ways be.
A life together with
you
is what means most to
me.
Take my hand in your
hand today,
And step with me to
forever,
And promise to be there
with me
And to leave me alone
never.
This is the promise we
shall make,
Two in a world not al-
ways fair,
Standing here with the
promise
of someone always to

love and care.

Wedding Band

I shall take, today, your
loving hand,
And you, my love, will
take mine.
We shall create a bond
together
Much stronger than all
of time.
I will always and truly
hold you
And you will always
hold me.
That's because I know
deep down inside
That our love will al-
ways be.
We complete a circle to-
gether.
We are one soul and one
heart.
And I pray to God high
up above
That we two should
never part.
Together, we shall face
all life's pains.
You will be there to hold
my hand.
Together, forever, just as
long
As I wear your wedding

band.

The Way Love

Love comes soft;
on angel wings,
on little cat feet.
Love comes quick;
on the heels of light-
ning,
on the taking of a
breath.
Love comes unseen;
on the sun's own rays,
on the heart's own
strings.
And so to me you
brought your love-
soft, quick, unseen.
One moment unclear,
the next like a crystal
view.

Turned Around

What are you doing to
me?
You've got me all turned
around.
I can't think straight
if I'm not thinking of
you
And even then it's all a
blur.
What are you doing to
me?
Please tell me because I
don't know.
All I know for sure is
that I don't know
and all I want is you.

The Sun Shown

As I slowly slide,
Slipping to a sunless
sea
from the sunlit sands,
So my soul sees and
hears
The sound of stars.
So, spirit, this for you
I sail on a ship of sacri-
fice
over the sunless sea,
Sea spray sullying my
shirt
Sighing, I see the sleep-
ing stars
in the sea of my soul.
So as sadness and sor-
row
tries to swallow me,
I say my sight for the last
sign.
So I seem to be in the
sunlit sand,
No sorrow or sadness do
I seek.
So the sun has begun to
shine
on the silent and sleep-
ing stars
in my selfless soul with
my secret spirit.

Eternal Lovers

Their love is eternal.
It lasts forever.
Lifetime after lifetime.
They find each other al-
ways.
They die together so
they may love again.
So one doesn't have to
wait too long.
In each life, they are
drawn to each other.
Their souls forever in-
tertwined.
They will love longer
than forever.
They can sense each
other
The scent of a thousand
or more years.
Their first meeting was
on the banks of the
Nile.
There they loved a for-
bidden love.
They would rather die
than be apart.
And they have died that
way,
many times.
They've been betrothed
to others,

And still they loved.
They were executed,
made   outcasts   and
lovers to others.
But they still loved only
the other.
The tie that binds them
extends forever.
For these two lovers
there isn't an end in
sight
for their love.

Eyes of Mine

In the eyes of the story-
teller,
There is a wisdom most
never know,
We can tell you any story
you wish,
And take you places
you'd never go.

The Seeking

The world expounds
upon her children
a life
and we live,
after a fashion.
Life that is not under-
stood.
Life that is not really
lived.

Kiss the heavens.
Kiss the stars.
Kiss the sun.
Let the fires
burn you
through and through
and prove
you are alive.
Turn eyes wide
to what is unknown
and seek the answer
when no one knows
the question.

Embrace the heavens.
Embrace the Stars.
Embrace the sun.
Answers to it all can be
found.
Hundreds of answers to
one question.

Finding the answer isn't
the chore,
finding the right answer
is.
There is only one answer
to everything.
The answer that is
found in yourself.
Seeking the answer in
others
leads you to their an-
swers,
not your own.
Open your eyes wide
to the truth
to the possibilities
to everything
you've never seen
and you'll see
there's a whole world
hidden
behind a glass veil.

Hold the heavens.
Hold the stars.
Hold the sun.
Seeking throughout
life
maybe I'll find the
Truth
at the end.

You Are My...Everything

Simple whispers in the
night
seek my ears as you are
there
and you will always be.
I knew from the begin-
ning
you were special.
A gift from whatever di-
vine spirit
resides   around   and
within us.
A heart can become
fragile
with all the fires,
even   stone   turns   to
glass.
By my side, there you
are.
By my side, you always
were.
A heart seeks another
in this forsaken world,
another to hold to,
another to cling to,
and in the hour of great-
est need,
something to grasp and
hold.
I could be shattered into

a million
sparkling pieces of sim-
ple sand,
and one touch from
you
would bring me back
whole again.
I could be melted down
into a pile
of molten formless
wax,
and one word from
you
would build me back
whole again.
I always knew this.
You are my soulmate.
No other is there for
me
down through the
ages;
you and I have been
one.
I've dreamed of you for
years
before you ever came to
me.
My stories, my words,
you were there,
though I thought it all
fantasy.
Fantasy can become
real...

Break the Bonds

Now you've broken me
apart,
from fragile glass down
to sand
tearing down my frac-
tured heart,
you shall never under-
stand.

How you've torn me
asunder
just to see what makes
up me,
and still you stare in
wonder
at what it is you now
see.

Bound tight to you, I
can't speak.
Bound tight to you, I
can't see.
Bound tight to you, I am
weak.
Bound tight to you, this
is me.

My body does not die
away,
and so you want to
know why.

So you take, and day by
day,
peel away my life, I
won't die.

Piece by piece and bit by
bit
you tear away just the
same.
Deep inside a fire lit
begins to burn, white
hot flame.

To break my bonds, I
will fight.
To break my bonds, to
be strong.
To break my bonds, this
tonight.
To break my bonds,
right the wrong.

No more can I take this
pain,
I will stand up against
you
before you drive me in-
sane,
And I know just what to
do.

As I Am

In another place,
In another time,
In another life,
I was as I am.

On Drowning

Remorse and sorrow
thick and vicious,
they course in my
veins,
real and red,
my life force.
What can I do
but lie down and die?
Can I live?
Or will my own pain
poison me
with its sick,
sweet,
metallic taste?
Oh, here it is,
it is
like drowning in blood
or anguish
they are one and the
same now.
The water, like so much
fluid
fills these lungs that are
so tangible
but is it real even now?
The air stops,
and there is a feeling,
like pressure in my
chest
and then everything
seems different

and it looks different.
There is a feeling of
peace now.
My head is light, and I'm
slipping away.
Falling deeper into this
pool
of my own making
but what is this?
Something…some-
thing….
I am floating in a pool
of…
of what?
Is it blood?
Is it water?
Is it even real?
I see a light
I see something
I see my salvation…
I'm reaching up
will you take my hand?

The Light

The sun has set,
And the moon will not
rise
to light my way.
I cannot see to find a
path
in this murky darkness
that is all around me.
Now, there is this small
light.
But from where does it
come?
Ah, I can see from where
it comes now.
It is coming from my
own self.
Now I understand.
A light can only shine
in the dark.

Falling Star

Inside my secret sky,
a star blazes bright.
I never asked why
it gives off my light.
without it, I'd die
because it is my sight.
That is all I know
and it is all I need.
One day I do grow
and learn that I lead.
It's gone if it ever ends,
and light once gone,
never mends.
the star will fall from my
sky,
and I shall die.

**From Natural to Arti-
ficial**

Natural people
spend their lives
trying to learn
and develop
all the things around
and everything
they want and
desire to become
and in the end they
simply are trying to
be real
but they end up
making their world
just to become
artificial people.

Poetical Fire

The *poeticus furor* swallows me.
I am in a world of my own creation.
Symbols and metaphors
and meanings
With my *currente calamo.*
For I have a *cacothus scribendi*
That is forever insatiable.
And I think,
Poeta nascitur, non fit.
So true, because I was.

Pages in a Book

Sending away my love
across
the chosen miles.
Thoughts of you in my
mind,
giving me many smiles.
Thinking of you so
much,
sending my mind reel-
ing.
What is this thing I
have?
What is this I'm feel-
ing?
Something I've never
felt.
Something I've never
known.
Is it love in my heart
from the seed that you
have sown?
I feel like I'm all new,
like I'm an open book,
and you are here to
read
the pages, take a look...

Be Burned

Touch the fire,
and be joyfully burned.
If you do not,
you will never live.
Let the blisters come,
Let them fester and
hurt,
And when they pop and
are no more
Feel the joy
that can only come after
pain.
So be brave, young
heart,
Step up to the fire
and begin to live.

Our Love

Our love is fresh
Like the dew on a
morning rose.
Our love is sweet
Like the chocolates on
Valentine's morn.
Our love is nurturing
Like the warmth of a
mother's touch.
Our love is changeful
Like the wind whisper-
ing in the night.
Our love is eternal
Like the endless stars
burning bright.
Meant to be,
Always will be,
Loving and Living
Forever in love.

First Kiss

Our lips meet,
and our souls touch.
In that instant
we are complete.
We separate and step
back,
the feeling fading.
We stare into each oth-
er's eyes
and we want to be whole
forever.
We want to stand to-
gether
through the winds of
time.
We want to be One.
We watch and wait.
Should we do this?
Should we become
whole?
We come together
again,
the decision made
the first time we came
together.
We will be whole.
We will be complete.

Learn

Into the deep, dark sea,
my life has gone.
There it will remain
until I learn to swim.

I Still Love You

In the midst of past hot
summer days,
Upon my bed, I've
dreamily laid.
There, I've seen your
face before my eyes,
And thought of you in a
world full of lies.

But I still love you.
Oh, how I love you.
And how I wish you
could be here, too,
Because I still love you.

When I had your eternal
and true love,
It always made me feel a
step above.
I felt like we were made
for each other,
I knew I would never
love another.

Oh, the truth is some-
thing I can no longer
hide,
I lost my heart and soul
on that night you died.
You have gone, though
for me, you did care

Now, I know, whoever
said life was fair?

But I still love you.
Oh, how I love you.
And how I wish you
could be here, too,
Because I still love you.

You know, I found your
picture yesterday,
I just looked at it and
tucked it away.
Tears came to my eyes,
and I didn't know what
to do,
So I stood there, eyes
closed thinking of you.

I still love you.
Oh, how I love you.

Falling Kiss

A kiss
is like a
velvet reminder
that we are but
half of a whole.
To remind us so
sweetly
that we are created
needing the other part
worse than we even
need ourselves.
To descend into the
abyss
of light that we seek
we need the other half.
So we have a kiss,
the meeting of lips
and souls
that tells us more
than something
as simple of a thing as
a bit of physical con-
tact
but a meeting of souls
and a flowing of spirit
from one to another.

In Truth—Beauty

Ivory skin,
Scarlet lips,
Azure eyes,
Flaxen hair.
Does that equal Beau-
ty?
Do the color of
skin, lips, eyes and hair
make her more beauti-
ful
than another?
Pale skin,
Red lips,
Blue eyes,
Yellow hair.
Is that less beautiful
now?
There are no flowers in
the words,
so are there any less
flowers in the
girl?
I say pale instead of
ivory,
I say red instead of scar-
let,
I say blue instead of
azure,
I say yellow instead of
flaxen.
They are all the same

words
for the same colors,
though the first has no
poetry.
Yet the first would
evoke
more an image of beauty
then the second.
Why is that?
Does poetry make it so
different?
Poetry becomes the ves-
sel
Of beauty.

In Twain

Take my hand
then rip out my heart
and give me your own.
What I am is an
image of you.
Then split my heart in
twain
and half for you
and half for me,
but neither will
ever be whole.

Heart's Fire

A fire is in my heart,
Forever burning there.
You can see a reflection
of that fire deep in my
eyes.
It has always been this
way
and it always will be this
way,
for the fire is as eternal
as my very soul.

In Her Eyes

She knows he's true.
She knows he loves only
her.
And as he stares into her
eyes,
He knows she loves only
him.
In her eyes.
He sees that she knows
the truth.
He knows he's her
love.
And she will be his for-
ever.

Home

Take me home.
Don't leave me here.
Home.
I can't stay here.
Home isn't a place.
I don't want to be here.
I want to leave this
place.
Take me home.
Please come get me.
Home is with you,
forever with you.

Flame of Fire

My soul is full of the
flame
of which I cannot
name.
And I try but cannot
tame.
Fire, ice, all the same.
I was changed when it
came.
If it leaves, then with
shame
would I live with a
chain
and lest I go insane
without hope, I cannot

feign
my life.

Creation

Art is something
relative.
Create with
paint,
music,
words.
All the same,
visual,
audio,
mental.
The effect is the same,
Art is born of each.

Day of Reckoning

This is the day.
The day of reckoning
has come.
I shall rise up against
Those who have taken
from me.
And I will strike
Those who have struck
me.
And it will be as they
say,
The oppressed shall
rise
Against the oppressors.

Soulfire

Fires
burning through eter-
nity
blister my flesh
and bring me ecstasy
once more.
A painted purple spirit
is set free as the fire
burns
deep within.
Lives pass like seconds
and what was young
becomes ancient.
The same fire burns
within these eyes as has
burned
for eternity.
Turn the eons to days
and turn the years into
breaths
and there you will find
me
a living and breathing
creature
once more.
Open wide wings of in-
substantial mist
and fly home again and
again.
Open wide wings of
thought and hope

and fly to me again and
again.
Touch my flesh
and feel the fire
that lies within.
That lays in wait.
For you.

One Moment

It can be said truly
that man must love.
But is that very love
vice or virtue?
Can it be said that all
love is pure?
Can it be said that all
love is not?
Neither can be said.
The love of friends
and the love of lovers
are one in the same.
Love can heal the
wounded
but it can wound the
healed as well.
The price for love is
pain.
Man does a great many
things for love.
Often good and often
bad.
So tell me truthfully,
will you take a lifetime
of pain
for one moment of pure
love.

ACT 2
DANCES OF DARKNESS

T he sun sinks behind the horizon, and the moon slowly becomes visible. Stars blink into existence, slowly filling up the black sky. Far away, the sounds of the theater can still be heard. But inside the small studio, the dancer has changed. No longer are her steps joyous and uplifted. She has begun to slow her pace, and the music around her has become slower and more somber.

Outside, the cold has begun to set in, and the mother frantically tries to calm her nursing baby against the wall in the abandoned business beside the studio. The little girl crouches against her mother, scared as each new night sound brings her closer to the scream that is building behind her tongue.

But even in the dark, the mother holds tight to hope, as tight as she holds to the babe suckling at her breast. There is something about him, his wide innocent eyes unknowing of the pain that life will bring. She stares up through the broken rafters at the moon dawning full in the sky and swears that she can hear soft and sad music coming from the building behind her. But esoteric instruments chime in, leaving the imagination filled with dread and foreboding, all save the light notes of a flute in the background.

The dancer nearly weeps as she moves, taking her to the floor, expanding and moving like water flowing and tears dripping into the night. The darkness is creeping, threatening to overcome every ounce of light in the world. Will there be no end to it? Will there ever again be another light?

The music again tells stories to her, stories without words. There is pain, both of broken hearts and lost loved ones. There are stories of woe from confusion, hatred, and misunderstandings. Sometimes, unfair events occur in the world around us, and the music tells tales of death and pain at the hands of others.

The dancer leaps and spins, though, still able to move despite the despair that can easily fall over her in the darkness. There are so many things in the darkness that can consume us all.

And the Heavens Wept

And the heavens them-
selves looked down and
wept
From sad skies gray rain
like bitter cold tears
As there she laid; she
eternally slept
Leaving us here now
with all of our fears.

A star divine had been
taken away
To return to burn bright
among the sky.
Leaving us here now to
live on each day
Without her true guid-
ing light

Oh
Keeping us all together
through it all
But now she has gone
For she waited.

Oh
But I must stand strong
for her guiding light-
It will aid me now each
day that I try

and it shall guide me
through the depths of
night.

The sky drops tears like
ice upon my head
And my face is wet from
more than the rain
But I will cherish the life
that she lead
As the very heavens
weep for our pain.

Liquid Blue Eyes

Teardrops fall like rain
Upon a clean glass
table
Forming little pools of
ocean.
Liquid blue eyes are
full of sorrowed pain
and
reigning fear
Unknowing of the fu-
ture's truth.
This one awaits anoth-
er
who does not come
And will not come
even after an ocean of
salt tears.

Ancient Song of the Exile

Sing
Sing the ancient mea-
sured rhyme.
Exile
Because it is my own.
We sing of these stories
they tell
So we stand all alone.
Sing
Sing that ancient song
with me.
Alone I am
Surely we can still fight
Even though from
home we are far.
We can try to make
right.
Sing
Sing the ancient words
till the end.
They will fight and try
to make us go
But we will spread our
word.
And make so many
more learn to know
How to break down the
ford.
Sing
Sing the ancient words

and die.

A Disease

Stay away.
Go away.
Never come near me.
I am poison to you.
Stay where you are
I am a disease in you.
I have no cure.
Don't come near me.
No
Don't come to me.
I am your pain
I am your hurt.
I don't want to hurt
you.
I'm telling you...
You never listen.
I'm warning you...
Oh
You'll die in my arms
again.

A Farewell to Inno-
cence

Till the time my life be-
gins
send me the dark
so that I may learn
what darkness is
so I may distinguish the
light.

Show me
what it means to be for-
saken
and seen with scorn by
those that were
once embraced with
love.

Teach me while I am still
safe
about the danger that
lies ahead.
Prepare me for my joy-
ous birth
by making me ready for
pain.
Tucked away so safe and
warm
I must be ready for the
cold to come.

Innocence of mine

for I am soon to be born.

Are You the Judge?

"Judge not,lest ye be
judged."
And here you sit you
judge.
When I speak you
judge.
When I walk you
judge.
When I live you judge.
When I change you
judge.
You're religious
You are not the judge.
There is one judge
And you are not that
judge.
My values are not for
you to judge.
My wants are not for
you to judge.
My needs are not for you
to judge.
My pains are not for you
to judge.
My loves are not for you
to judge.
You are not my judge
We all have the same
judge.
And when you come
before that judge

Will they deem you a
sinner?

The Bell That Tolls

In the silence
and no one on earth can
hear.
In the darkness
and all I can do is fear.

I am so very afraid
of this deal that was
made.
For life I would gladly
trade
the cold tomb where I
am laid.

What waits for me after
this?
I will just cease to exist.
I'll lay shrouded in the
mist.
Death hath given me his
kiss.

In the silence
and although I really
tried
In the darkness
and silently I have died.

Endless Nights

Endless days and nights
are all I have.
But the nights are
longer.
My eyes are wide open
though I should be fast
asleep.
I really have no reason to
sleep.
If I go to sleep
and why should I want
to wake to face
another lonely day.
My family and friends
are all gone.
I do wish they were
here.
There is nobody here.
All who were here are
dead.
Everyone is gone that I
ever loved.
They wanted to hurt me
worse than death.
They took everything I
loved and destroyed it.
They won't kill me.
They let me suffer in
pain.
I walk this world alone.
I wish sometimes that I

could just die.
I probably will if I keep
this up.
I don't sleep or eat or
drink.
I just sit up night after
night
watching the hours pass
me by.
Days seem more like
years
as I make my slow way
through
lonely days and endless
nights.

Through My Open Window

I left the window open
last night
and death crept in
silently.
He came to take me far
away
but I fought him
valiantly.

I did not really want to
go
it did no good that I
tried,
that I fought to stay and
live,
be still, toll the bell, I've
died.

Lack of Life

The world is choking
Dying of lack of air.
And life is air,
so it is dying of lack of
life.
That is,
real and true living life.

The Dragon's Fire

My life is over now, I'm
dying.
No one will tell me but I
know.
I'm sitting against
a cement wall patterned
with red
and I'm sitting in a thick
crimson pool.
How could I not be dy-
ing?
I reach down and touch
the numb spot
just below my breast-
bone.
I raise my shaking hand
up to my
unfocused eyes.
And I stare amazed at
the
dark red blood dripping
from it.

I look up and around at
the
blurring faces that
stare with morbid fasci-
nation.
I hear sirens, but are they
going away?
Are they going to leave

me to die?
Tears come now,
mixing with the blood
flowing freely from my
mouth.
I won't live to see eigh-
teen.
I won't even live to see
tomorrow's sun rise to
light fire to the sky.
I was going to do so
much in life.

There is a girl child
standing   above   me
now.
This is her house.
Blonde hair...
it looks like a corona of
fire to me
as the lightning strikes
and lights up the world
around us.
She seems to bring me
peace,
what is this?

There is a boy standing
above me now.
He has a silver and black
gun
in his shaking hand.
The gun still smokes like
a dragon
sated with the brave

knight's blood.
His twelve year old face
is full of fear.
He cries so like a baby.
But a baby he is not.
Not with the dragon he
holds in his hand,
and in his heart.

...I'm so sorry
...will you forgive me
...the bullet wasn't
meant for you
...you just got in the
way
...it was another I meant
to kill
...it was my first shoot-
ing
...you have to under-
stand
...*perdoname*
...forgive me
...*mi dios*
...what have I done
...I didn't mean to kill
you....

I look up at him
and so does the angel to
my side.
The rain threatens to
choke me,
or is that my blood?
I cough,

and I see spatters fly
from my lips
to the face of my young
murderer.

My sweet angel child
whispers to him.
Or is she yelling?
I don't know...
The words are so dim.

...you wanted to kill
...you did kill
...why would you want
such a thing
...are you happy now
...look what you have
done
...it doesn't matter who
you wanted to kill
...look at her
...you did this
...are you proud
...are you happy
...you've killed your first
time
...does it make you feel
better
...the dragon you hold
has eaten you alive...

I look at him,
and hold out a shaking
bloody hand.
The police have come,

and the world has gone
silent.
I can't hear the thunder
any longer.
The red haze is thick
but I can still see them
cuff his slack wrists
as tears flow down his
face.

...please
...say you'll forgive me
...I wasn't going to kill
you
...please
...oh God
...please
...don't let this be.
...I wasn't going to kill
you...

I glance at my angel
as the rain begins to
fall,
washing the blood from
my body
and it runs down the
walk,
onward to a storm
drain.
There are sprinkles of
blood on her angel
face,
her sweet seven year old
angel face.

She does not move,
she only holds my
hand.

I was going to live.

My murderer's eyes go
wide
and he begins to
scream
as he is dragged away.
The paramedics are
running
but they are too late.
Sweet angel,
named Esperanza Luz,
you truly are my Light of
Hope,
mi angelita, my angel.
I close my eyes.
And peace envelopes
me.

And a Little Child Shall
Lead them.
May that Angel by *mi
Angelita*.

Secrets of the Dark

Fate turned blind yes-
terday
and now the world is
dark.

whirling and spinning
in the dark.

they come now and
then.
I hear the rattle of keys.
and then they all leave.

No voice, not any
more.
it left my throat long
ago
after the screaming was
done.
No hope, not any
more.
it left my heart long ago
after the crying was
done.

I see only the dark.
it is my second skin,
comforting my broken
heart
and teaching me its se-
crets.

The secrets of the dark.

twenty steps across the
back
then twenty steps up
each side
and eight steps to the
door
four steps across the
door
and another eight steps
to the side again.

all I need they said.
here I have come to my
end
and I think they hoped I
would die.

they were wrong.
I live to show them I am
strong.
I don't bend.
I don't break.
I will simply fade.
But not away.
I learn

The secrets of the dark.

There is no light.
And my eyes have
learned
to see through it.

and soon I will learn
all of the ways of dark-
ness
I will leave
and they will be at my
mercy.

I think I should close
them up
in a tiny space like this
but I won't give them
the darkness,
No I can't do that
because they might
learn

The secrets of the Dark.

Death of the Child

The child inside me died
today.
He sent her far away.
I am too young to be
without her.
I'm not all grown up
yet.
Yet my childhood is
gone,
there is no more.
My innocence was taken
from me,
and I don't know why.
It was all I really had.
And he took it away.
I lay crying in an alley-
way
I cry not for my own
pain,
but the child that is
dead.
In killing the child, he
almost killed me.
As a man, such a kind
man, lifts me up,
I look at his hands and
scream.
crouching into a small
space.
I curl up and weep, cry-
ing out,

She's dead; she's dead, so
cold and dead.
They come and take
me away in a screaming
van.
Why did he have to kill
the child
When I need her so
much?

Angel's Errand

I do not want to go this
time.
Sometimes it hurts so
much.
But I must go.
She's young and inno-
cent,
And she's dying.
So I must retrieve her to
heaven,
But the boy that de-
stroyed her will re-
main.
Though his life has been
destroyed as well,
Because he must still
live.
He must live with his
guilt,
But he'll never drink
again.
He will live guilty,
She will die innocent...
Now I must explain
That she is the lucky
one,
For tonight, she will sing
with the angels,
And her murderer shall
cry in pain,
with his own demons...

Not Yet

I see peace in the eyes of
a child,
an innocence untainted
by hate
made by adults and their
falseness.
Adults and their adult
ways.
Adult lies and adult
ideals.
None has tainted a
child.
Not yet has it spoiled
another generation.

Finality

Time's up
its ending
going away
and so am I.

No One Asked Her Why

She sat alone.
There was dirt under her
fingernails.
No one asked her why.
Her eyes were sunken
and hollow.
No one asked her why.

She shivered as the wind
blew.
But the shiver re-
mained
long after the wind was
gone.
People passed her
again and again.
Paying no heed to her
or the clothes that were
ripped
and torn.

A girl met a boy,
and they fell in love like
no others.
They wished to spend
their lives
simply loving each oth-
er.
They planned to mar-
ry,

and to solidify their
love
to make it all real.

Still, she sat alone.
She was pale in a sickly
way.
No one asked her why.
Her hair was stringy and
unkempt.
No one asked her why.

Soon enough a man
came into the room.
She looked up,
moving for the first
time.
He laughed and spoke
with his friends.
And this pallid girl
smiled a fetid smile.
She pulled the clothes
around her chest.

His hands on her,
holding her down,
pressing her into the
ground.
Then they shot him
and made him watch
as they slowly killed her
little by little.

And she sat alone.
Her smile was dead and

empty.
No one asked her why.
She stood then and went
to those she sought.
No one asked her why.

She stumbled away from
the place,
screams following her
and blood on her hands
still.
Around her the night
encroached
and she felt the tears of
life leave.
She felt that her job was
done
but still the memories
flashed
now with their own.

They cut him and hurt
him
as they did horror to
her.
His blood flowed to the
ground,
and she tasted it
and her anger screamed
so that she did not stay
dead
until her vengeance was
sated.

She walked alone.

Her spirit yearning to
rest forever.
No one asked her why.
Her heart broken
through by the hor-
rors.
No one asked her why.

She reached the grave
where her body had not
remained.
Her hands rested on the
stone,
and she called out to
someone.
She sat down in the fresh
dirt
with her back to the
stone that said her
name.
A vision came to her of
her love,
and she reached up and
embraced him.

They came and dug
fresh graves
for those that had done
so wrong.
The vengeance of a
ghost killed them
it is said that night
but still there is no one
that is sure.
Rapists and murderers

they were,
all knew it for certain.

She was no longer
alone.
Her body was undis-
turbed that they could
tell.
No one asked why.
The grave was covered
and packed, so
No one asked why.

No Turning Back

Gangs, violence, drugs,
Alcohol, hatred, greed,
Homicide, suicide.
Alone they are danger-
ous.
Together   they   are
lethal.
You start with one,
Then there's another,
and another.
And you keep going,
until its way past too
late.
You've   reached   the
end.
You just can't go farther
than death.
You can't come back.
No second chances.
Use your mind,
Think about your ac-
tions.
Don't   destroy   your
body.
Keep your soul free of
hate.
And love your brothers
and sisters.
And you will set your
spirit free.
Don't die for any reason

that is
meaningless,
You can't come back.
And somewhere, some
when,
someone needs you.

No Black Robes

Black robes, you have
not.
But you think you do.
You look at me,
judge, jury, and execu-
tioner if need be
and you do commit the
sin.
Man is not to judge.
Only God may judge.
You are not God,
and yet you still try to
judge me.
Upon my death,
I will not have your sin
of pretending to be
judge.
I know how it will be for
me
when I am judged I will
not fear.
I've been judged all my
life already.
How will it be for you?
How will you, the sin-
ner, be judged?

No More

In this life of mine,
I only wish to live,
To be left alone.
I have no more to give.
You are always here,
And I want you to go.
I want you to leave.
Why, I do not know.

ACT 3

DANCES OF SHADOWS

D ances are eternal. At least, they are for the Shadow Dancer. But after the light and darkness have passed, she is left in the place of shadows. Shadows are essential because there must be light, but to be light, there must be darkness. And in between the two lies the shadow realm. Some call this the realm of dreams and imagination, but what is it except a feral reflection of the soul? The dancer's music changes once more.

There is a discordant sound here and there, clashing tones and unreal-sounding melodies. Cymbals, low and long bassoon notes, and high-pitched piccolo sounds offend the ears and make one wonder what is happening. To dance, there are jaunty moves, some smoother than others, frantic pace, and slow pace. The dance is as unpredictable as the music it accompanies.

In the night world of dreams, a man dreams of his friends and then watches them as they are torn away from him by their enemies in war. A little girl snuggles with her father, then watches as he is eaten alive by a monster that lives within him. A down-on-her-luck mother screams in horror as her baby and remembers her father's voice when he told the most amazing bedtime stories. The mother remembers her sick husband holding their baby for the first and last time. The look on his face would light her life forever.

The dancer is neither sad nor happy, but she feels surreal headiness, and the music and the dance bring her into a strange, unknown world. The mirror reflects strange flashes of light and droplets of darkness among the great shadows around her. She herself has become one of the shadows in which she dances.

The   Storm   Has Come

Whispers of wind whis-
tle soft in my ear,
wicked   waves   wash
upon   the   cold   white
shore
and now I find that I can
wait no more,
for you have come not to
dissuade my fear.

Alone along the sands of
time, they leer
at me; I stand upon the
wings of lore,
the storm will chill me
to the darkened core;
I know it was you who
brought me to here.

Storming,   blowing
upon   red   and   white
sand,
I shall lose my life to the
storm above,
into its harsh winds, my
weak soul shall flee,
rising up and away from
this cruel land;

You would forsake me

too, my own sweet
love.
Forget who it was that I
was to be.

The Ending is the Beginning

The tree not to break
must first bend.
My life to begin must
first end.

Find what you will in
the life that I lead,
In the dark, I only search
for a light.
Chaos surrounds me,
but I fill my need,
Though death chases
me in the endless night.

With a wish upon a
star,
I will send myself far.

I don't just run from
those who pursue me,
I turn on them, and I
give them their fight.
I teach them not to re-
turn to my sight.
They leave me then, for a
while, and leave me be.

One day, wish I may
wish I might,
My soul shall rise up and

take flight.

Death closes in close
each and every day
but I escape it with my
ample skill.
My eyes are wide even at
night while I lay.
Holding on to my life by
my sheer will.

I will wish myself simply
to die,
For I have lived naught
but in a lie.
Day by day the end is
drawing quite near.
I stare up and smile at
the sky.

Out of this hell, I shall
rise and fly
and I really don't feel
any fear.
If wishes were horses
with wings,
I would fly head up, and
the world sings.

Praise to all that came
before me in the dark
paved my way, built the
bridge so I don't fall.
They did what they had
to and left their mark,

I will ascend on past
mere life in all.

So the life can begin, it
ends.
So the tree does not
break; it bends.

Three Elements

—Angel of the Air
Breath of wind like
rain,
Carry me away on high
and make me alive.

—Dewdrop Tears
Dewdrop tears fall
down
upon a moist earth
bared here
for a rain of soil.

—Cycle
The world moves on-
ward
though the flower shall
wither
and return to dust.

Emotion

Falling fast,
Deep into a well of emo-
tion.
Tears, fears, pains,
loves.
They are liquid around
me.
Sights to my eyes,
Beauty, horrors, awe-
some, awful.
I see it all
On the span of my hori-
zon.
In the taking of a
breath,
I feel all around,
Emotions run ram-
pant.
Love, hate, anger, fear.
I feel it so strong,
Happiness, loss, hope,
despairs.
It is all right here.

Twisting Free

Twisting into the wind
my heart thrums
inside a maelstrom
like a bolt that cannot
be
harnessed
On a midsummer's
night
sky.

Brilliant black velvet
illuminating ebon cur-
tain
and eyes like diamonds
sparkle and shine

The air smelled of lilac.

Into free whispers,
a soul of sweet lavender
bloomed.

In the Harlequin's Touch

Simple.
Sweet.
I feel the cool
Harlequin touch.
What do I do?
When the joke's
on the fool?

Bitter.
Complex.
Multiple colors strike
the mirror in the
darkest night
of a soul lit by the star
of solitude.

Salty.
Simple.
Tears of joy
and of sorrow mix
upon this toy
within my hands
so fragile
and glass.

I am the harlequin
and the bells ring on
as the white paint
drips in a rain of salty,
bitter

dreams,
but still, they are sweet
to some tongue.

My Dream of Life

Water
drip and flow
ebb and know

Dreams like eddies,
time like rivers,
This is the touch of
emotion
that fills my heart like
the ocean.

Fire
crack and burn
mark and learn

Thoughts like blazes,
memories like infer-
nos;
This is the version of my
name
that fills my soul with
the flame.

Air
whip and blow
slip and know

Hopes like winds,
desires like heavens,
This is how I shall die
that fills my spirit with

the sky.

Earth
join and turn
stay and learn

Plans like mountains,
views like canyons;
This is the unending
semblance of sound
that fills my mind with
the ground.

Protector of the Unicorn

A pure white vision sits
with a horn of gold,
sits beside a lake
of pure, clear water.

A red fire-breathing giant
sits above,
keeping watch, vigilant,
protector of the fragile
creature below.

None shall harm the unicorn
because the dragon
watches.

Of Today

Since today has come,
What shall we say of it?
Praise it?
Curse it?
I know not what to say,
for to speak
Tis binding.

Here Hear

Turn me into naught
but an idle idol.
Tis inseparable
from truth.
No words mean any-
thing.
No sounds find my
ears.
The world is falling
dead lands
of hatred
of cruelty
of distrust
of destruction.
Tis not the end it is
true.
No, I'm here.
No one hears.

The Dreamer

Reaching across time,
Entombed in a world
apart,
The dreamer touches
me.

As I accept this touch,
I think,
Should I allow this

touch?

Too late, I scream no.
But letting go of the
dreamer isn't possible.
And now I cannot.
Out of time, I'm
pulled,
and the dreamer is free.

I'm reaching out to ask
if you
will accept my touch.
Will you accept
the beauty and the pain
Of being trapped and
alone?
Will you chance and
Touch the dreamer
to become the dreamer?

Watercolor Dreams

My eyes opened this
morning
from a dream of soft and
pastel.

Once more, the world is
in black and white
with a few shades of gray
in between.
My heart sank through
shades of blue
and paused at a beauti-
ful violet
only to continue on to
rest on a
dark gray.

I cannot continue like
this.
Without color what is
there?
No one listens to me.

Everyone around me
plies the grays.
They make everything
without life.
Without color,
how can they walk?

Black and white.

Right or wrong.
Death or life.
And the shades of gray
in between.

But it's all different in
my
watercolor dreams.

There, life is rampant
with color
and beauty creeps in the
strangest places.
Faces of color
change the world
and the world of color
changes them.

But I'm the only one
who dreams
in   my   watercolor
dreams.
Everyone else is content
with
their simple black and
white
and shades of gray.
But even in the shad-
ows,
some colors live.

How can I survive
breathing gray
when my soul needs yel-
low and blue?

How can I live eating
black and white
when I hunger for red
and green?
How can I endure such
simplicities
when I need the com-
plexities?
They all turn away.

They all don't want to
hear.
I'm   talking   about
changing their lives,
and they are content
right here.
They don't want to turn
away
to something more liv-
able.
They want the simple.
They want the comfort-
able.
They want the steady.

So I guess it will never
change,
I'm stuck here inside my
quiet dreams.

**Mr. White and the
Seven Children**
A Modern-Day Fairy

Tale...or Not

Mr. White.
with pressed perfect
pinstripes
white and black
smells of starch in the
morning
and of cigars in the
evening.

[Knocking, Knocking]

The door is old and fad-
ed wooden
and distaste crosses a
face smooth
and kept up with mois-
turizers
each and every day.
A hand fears a splinter
in its perfect, unmarred
appearance
and manicured and lac-
quered nails
recoil.

[Knocking, Knocking]

Inside, seven children
stir.
Inside, seven souls
burn.
Inside, seven hearts
break.

Inside, seven spirits
yearn.

[Knocking, Knocking]

The door creaks open,
and he barges into a
small
dark room.
Inside they all move
around,
as dirt and soot cling to
them
even this long after leav-
ing work.
They don't whistle.

[Mr. White]
Gather children,
round yon dirty seat.
must speak with you
of your conditions,
and bring me food to
eat.

[Scrambling, Scram-
bling]

all is set down,
and the children sit
facing this immaculate
man
as he scrunches his
nose
at the plain toast

on the yellow melamine
plate.

[Mr. White]
No parents have you
yet.
And no parents will you
have.
You will continue
to work here for us
since no one wants any
of you.

[Dawn]
A   child   of   golden
blonde hair,
And quiet blue eyes,
She stares at the man be-
fore her,
Her dirty face was open
to lies.
Mr. White,
We have needs,
Will you not listen?

[Mr. White]
Oh, tell me, pray tell...

[Hungry]
He is thin and drawn,
And   his   shoulders
shake
As before him, he
speaks.
He speaks for his own

sake.
Sir, we have no food
here,
once we ate at school,
but they've taken that
even away.

[Mr. White]
Bah, haven't you heard,
boy?
Children are too fat to-
day.
You don't need free food
on us.

[Sickly]
She is also thin and
drawn,
but there is more than
hunger here.
Her body is in pain, and
more
as for her life she does
fear.
Sir, there is no more
medicine.
How should I get well so
I may work,
since you've quit send-
ing us help?

[Mr. White]
Bah, girl, don't you
know?
You should have done

more before
but now you aren't
worth the time.

[Needy]
His clothes are rags and
ribbons,
and he looks quite the
fright
as he's not changed his
clothes
for many days and
nights.
Sir, there are no clothes
for us.
How shall I make more
money
when no one will give
me a job?

[Mr. White]
Bah, boy, none of my
concern.
I won't give you money
so that you
might go out and make
more money for me.

[Lonely]
A forlorn-looking thing,
he sits hunched
around himself so much
alone
all he really wants is even
one person

to take the time to call
him on the phone.
Sir, all I want is someone
to call my own,
a family to love me and
take care of me,
and be with me always.

[Mr. White]
Bah, boy, haven't you
heard?
It's far cheaper for
everyone to go out
and adopt a foreign
child before you.

[Thirsty]
A girl who is quite short
and thin,
she appears to have
bright eyes
and she looks to have
one aim,
to blaze a trail in her own
right.
Sir, I want only to be
granted knowledge,
to be able to learn and
make my way,
and be taught the things
that I need?

[Mr. White]
Bah, girl, it doesn't con-
cern me.

You do fine at hard labor
and all,
and knowledge is power,
not for you.

[Empty]
His eyes are drooping
down,
and there are many
things
that once he wanted,
but now
There is no reason to
reach brass rings.
Sir, there is no reason to
better,
even if we could, the fu-
ture holds nothing,
for all that we put in will
be gone.

[Mr. White]
Bah, boy, don't you
know?
You should have worked
harder
And then the future
would be brighter.

[Dawn]
You've left us no
choice.
You won't give us food.
You won't give us medi-
cine.

You won't give us
clothes.
You won't give us
homes.
You won't educate us.
You won't give us a fu-
ture.
So we will see your true
self.

[Tinkling, Tinkling]

With that, she picked
up a stick and swirled
around,
and she became a
fairy-type creature.
she wears a dress of crys-
tal shards
and her blond hair flows
around her head
and her blue eyes sparkle
with light.
she stands tall over the
children
who stare up at her with
wonder.
She then tapped Mr.
White on the head.

[Hungry] Mr. White,
what long nose you
have.
[Sickly] Mr. White,
what big ears you have.

[Needy] Mr. White,
what large feet you
have.
[Lonely] Mr. White,
what gray skin you
have.
[Thirsty] Mr. White,
what tiny eyes you
have.
[Empty] Mr. White,
what loud noise you
make.

Before them stood a
gargantuan creature,
the ripped shreds of a
pinstripe suit
still smelling of fresh
starch.
He looked around, his
eyes livid,
as his proper form had
been revealed.
He trumpeted loudly
his anger
and stomped out of the
house,
leaving a large hole in the
wall.

[Dawn]
Worry not, children,
come with me.

[Waving, Waving]

In the room ap-
peared six creatures with
wings,
and Dawn placed a child
on each one.
The creatures began to
fly away with her
to the new home of the
children.
Who would have
thought donkeys could
fly?
The children laughed as
rainbows spread across
the sky.

Eternal Nights

Into her mind begins a
single thought,
Heavy, and empty, it
sinks just like a stone
to the depths of dark-
ness; it's what she
sought.
Naught to escape her
live lips save a moan.

Dropping away into the
deep, dank dark
she has slipped deep into
the blood-red haze
and no more will she
ever leave her mark
trapped forever more in
this deadly daze.

Lost she is, a thing of her
own making
as she wanders as one
among the dead
paying the price for her
life-forsaking,
but always knowing the
life she had led.

The eternal night will be
her domain
and now, nothing will

ever be the same.

The Hunters

I am in the realm of
fear,
And I am waiting for
you.
I am one of the
hunters.
We will hunt you down
and pray on your fear.
You cannot escape us.
You will not escape us.
We seek out the weak
first.
But even the strongest
fall.
If you can survive here,
You can surely survive
anywhere.
And you will join us.
You will become the
prey,
Or you will become the
predator.
I became a hunter.
Now I lie in wait for
you,
Wondering,
Will you die like so many
others?
Or will you be strong
enough to join our
ranks

And become a Hunter?

Dark Dance

She was walking alone.
She was the poison he
was seeking.
She was the death he
wanted.
She was happy to
oblige.

He was walking alone.
He was looking for
trouble.
He was looking for his
end.
He was happy to find
her.

She was a beautiful fe-
line,
slick, black, and shiny.
Sensuous   curves,
melodic voice,
snow white skin, raven
hair,
coral red lips, and blood
red finger tips.
She was like his dream.

Dancing, her dress was
black, second skin.
He felt infinite death
radiate from her like

perfume.
It draws him deeper.
Like a cobra, she dazzles
him with her dance.
He barely has time to
notice the mark upon
her neck, his
kisses have revealed
before she has taken him
into the dark,
her own forever.

Deafening Tones

Drops of water
falling so softly
with an equally soft
sound.
Do you hear?
Or does it deafen you
beyond your capacity?

Flames of fire
flickering so loudly
with an equally loud
sound.
Do you hear?
Or does it deafen you
beyond your capacity?

To be deafened by
loud and soft,
hot and cold,
for all eternity.

Complete Immersion

He hears the call,
He knows she's there,
ready for him,
waiting alone for him
down there.

He leans over the ship's
rail,
and stares down into the
deep.
His shipmates watch
him carefully,
They all think,
The see is hungry to-
day
it wants him to keep.

Her bodice is alluring to
him,
he wants to be with
her,
and she wants him to be
with her,
and this is what she sings
to him.

His shipmates pull him
away,
and he cries out; he
wants to go.

His mates take him
down below,
to protect him,
they lock him down,
How can they know?

He mourns his lost
chance,
for he'll not get out
now,
but she sings to him
still.
Maybe there's a way, but
how?

He calls out to his
mates,
and he tells them he's
fine,
It's just a bit of crazi-
ness
brought on by the sea.
And he goes above to
the rail
where he sees the sea
shine.

He smiles in joy, for he
sees her,
below the surface, her
scales in green,
and he leans over,
she is the most beauti-
ful
creature he's ever seen.

He looks around for one
last time,
and vaults over the rail
into the sea,}
and he hears the sound
of voices
as he sinks way down
deep,
But just as he thinks he's
lost,
he is wrapped up in arms
and green,
Forever a lover of the sea.

crystal butterfly

Exhale
pale blue breath
tinged with frost.

Sometimes,
I'm so cold inside
I feel like I've simply
died.

Eyelashes drop snow
as diamond tears
tinkle and crash at my
feet
and all around me
flies the crystal butter-
fly
in which my soul
resides.

The ice encrusts a heart
that forgot how to beat
a long time ago,
and I can't remember,
what was it like
to be warm?

slip away
slip into the frigid wa-
ters
of my spirit that has
drowned in the world

as away flew the butter-
fly
of crystal ice.

I cannot catch it.
My hands are so slow
and cold
they do not work so
quickly
as it flies away from me.

Shattered ice piles at my
feet,
refracting the colors of
the sky.
Pale blue and yellow and
white.

The sun comes.
It brings light and
warmth,
the butterfly will melt
away
when the sun's warmth
floods the world.

water falls from the sky
in thick, heavy drops,
as I watch the butterfly
fly towards the warmth
of the sun
only to fall back down,
its wings melting away,
and my shattered soul
reforms.

Sometimes
I'm so warm inside
I feel as though I have
lived.

inhale
vivid yellow breath
tinged with the fire of
life.

The Straw That Burns

Crack, snap, pop.
The fire burns up the
straw.
It chews it up like a hun-
gry beast.
This is the last of the
un-charred land.
But it won't stand much
longer.
Ah, there it goes.

It all burned up,
Like so much straw.
It all fell,
Like so much debris.

The great cities did not
stand.
They fell right over
into the flames,
burning straw.

Stricken Candy

Enter the Ending.
Leave the Beginning.

Let us all kiss and cud-
dle
the dark spot on the
world
known as the oblivion.

Has it eaten us up?
Like a piece of ambrosia
for lies?
Stricken with poison on
our tongue?
Has it left us out in the
surging rain?
Only to return to find us
alive?
Against all odds?

Let us all fight and
pummel
the light spot on the
world
known as the oblivion.

Leave the Ending.
Enter the Beginning.

The Descent of a Malevolent

I stand and watch and
wait.
There's too much hurt
and hate.
How can I show and
prove
that love the world can
move?

They all hurt and hate
and make war.
They do so much and
are so unfair
to those few with the
will to care.
How can I show what it
is for?

How can I?
Is there hope?
Should I try?
Is there hope?
Can they cry?
Is there hope?

Can I teach them how to
truly live?
Can they understand
true life?
Can they really know

peace and love?
Or is it too late?
Can I teach them what it
means to give?
Can I make them stop
the strife?
And can I change their
fate?

What am I supposed to
do?
Should I stop and save
them all?
Or should I leave them
in hell?
I smile, and my heart
does tell.
I must stay and stop
their fall.
I will descend to change
you.

Will they see?
Is there hope?
Can they be?
Is there hope?
Hope's in me.
There is hope.

Ah, they will learn,
and I will be there.
They will learn to care,
Or they will burn.

Yes, I will bring them

hope indeed.
and my voice they had
better heed,
for if they fail to listen to
me
I will make them know
what hell can be.
They cannot take care
on their own
now they shall reap what
they've sown.

They'll   listen   to
teacher
and learn to live
or they will not live at all.

The Pen

I am writing.
And I am alone.

My pen frightens me to
death.

The ink is red, and I hate
it.
I have to draw on the
only ink I have.

I wouldn't write,
but I must.
I have to write.
I would not survive if I
did not.
But the only ink I have,
and the only ink my pen
can use
is difficult to draw.

I only wanted to write,
why must I be cursed?

Each morning,
I must draw more ink,
thick and viscous
from my own veins.
My ink,
my blood,
fills my pen.

I am alone,
with a lifetime of paper
and an eternal pen,
but I have no ink.

This pen,
it must have my life.
I open my veins,
and pour it out each
day
into the pen,
and then pour my life
onto the paper.

I am a true writer.
I pour my life out for my
words.

Papers,
so many papers,
covered with rusty red
marks.

I hate this pen.

But I have to write to
stay alive,
but as I write, it slowly
kills me.

I shall write forever,
in this cycle of dying and
living.

Oblivion—To Life

Oblivion.
Darkness enfolding.
Darkness I'm holding.

The light bleeds away
before my eyes,
and without knowing it,
it fades from the skies.
The black velvet wings
stretch out for me,
and then the light is
gone, and I see.

Darkness   never-end-
ing.
Darkness   ever   bend-
ing.

My touch brings about
the smoke black
and there is no way to
bring the light back.
The mists of the ending
ebb and flow
as I bring the darkness I
know.

Darkness I'm seeing.
Darkness I'm being.
Oblivion.

I am the ending of
everything
(and nothing)
I am the beginning of
nothing
(and everything)

Everything, everything
blackens at my touch.
[Everything, everything
blossoms at my touch.]
Everything, everything
withers off too much.
[Everything, everything
blossoms   up   too
much.]
Everything, everything
dies at my feet.
[Everything, everything
lives at my feet.]
Everything, everything
senses my retreat.
[Everything, everything
weeps at my retreat.]

The death...
[The life...]
Stop it all.
[Start it all.]

One last breath
leads to
One first breath.

Sweet blackness en-

fold,
bring me oblivion
sweet nothing | Every-
thing
sweet death. | Life

[From the blackness,
from the Oblivion
the light of life…
is born.]

The Stopping, Part One□

The grass is dead.
The ground is cracked.
There has been no wa-
ter
For many years.

The sun has been out
since a time ago.

Baked earth,
hard and dry,
constant light and
heat.
A barren wasteland in
which
nothing survives.

What happened?
No one knows.
No one cares.

The only care
is survival,
nothing more.
On the other side...

The Stopping, Part Two□

The grass is dead.
The ground is molded.
There has been so much
water
For many years.

The sun has been gone
since a time ago.

Damp earth,
soft and wet,
constant   dark   and
cold,
A soggy wasteland in
which
nothing survives.

What happened?
No one knows.
No one cares.

The only care
is survival,
nothing more.

Perfect Life...not Really

Perfection surrounds us
all.
From this height we
shall not fall.

Mary had a little lamb
Whose fleece was white
as snow,
And everywhere that
Mary went
The lamb was sure to
go.

The lamb in us has been
brought out.
We are now so meek and
mild.
Those who tamed us
brought this about.
We are no longer so
wild.

Mary still has her small
lamb
Whose fleece is not like
snow,
But it follows Mary all
day
no chance where she
may go.

We follow our orders, as
we should
and we live in peace to-
day.
We don't ever do what it
is we would
if we were free, we
aren't, nay.

Mary's lamb has grown
up big,
its fleece with blood is
red,
pulled with hurt and
hate, this lamb
and it will soon be
dead.

They've changed all of a
sudden now,
they hurt us and make
us bleed.
Now we take the pain
and wonder how
we can hurt them like we
need.

Mary's lamb has grown
tired
of all the hurt and pain.
It will soon turn on
Mary,
it has become quite
sane.

We have turned on
wolves full of rage
at those who tamed us
and took
our lives and put is in
this dark cage,
they should not hurt
lambs, just look.

Mary's lamb has many
teeth
made to tear Mary's
heart,
and its mouth is full of
blood,
oh, it has torn her
apart.

Their perfection is long
lost,
The wolves have paid
the cost.

Painted Roses

There hangs a paint-
ing.
Reds and pinks and
greens.
Painted Roses on the
wall.

Darkness encroaches
and I feel it coming to
me.
I cannot resist him.
The scarlet rush upon
my lips.
It is too quick and fast.
But the hunger must be
quenched.

The painting is my
own.
Colors of life etched
there as
Painted Roses on the
wall.

Living once long ago,
my heart burning with
passion
and it pumped my life
inside me.
Embraced by the
night,

A   crimson   flood
stemmed now,
after the dark to me as
his lover.

The painting is still
there.
I cannot take it down
any more.
Painted Roses on the
wall.
Everything now is dark
and lightless,
after I wed the night,
in an embrace of a crim-
son kiss.
I could never return to
before.
Now shrouded in his
love and death.
I am one with the dark-
ness.

But still there hangs my
life,
all that remains of my
life.
Painted Roses on the
wall.

The Great Dragon Encounter

A dragon approaches
the village.
They all run and scur-
ry.
They send their bravest
men
to their death, calling
Kill the dragon.
It has not done any-
thing.

A young woman is tak-
en.
A maiden must be sacri-
ficed
to the dragon and he'll
leave.
She's tied up and taken
to the dragon's lair and
left.

Please don't kill me as
you've killed so many.
I've only killed those
who would kill me.

Soon the maiden came
running back to the vil-
lage.
The dragon was seen

passing over the village.

Why are you here now?
What did the dragon
do?

He did nothing,
Said he was going
home
and to leave him alone.

Robes and the Rubber Band

The days of peace are
gone.
The days of love are
gone.
The days of hope are
gone.
The days of faith are
gone.

So these are the
robes that we fear.

The days of war are
here.
The days of hate are
here.
The days of loss are
here.
The days of hell are
here.

So these are the
robes that we don.

Blood is in red,
Truth is in blue.
Hatred is gray,
But this I knew.

My robes used to be so

blue,
Bright and bold in every
light,
Once so good and right
and true.
So the wrong turned
into right,
My robes have turned
red, I knew
It was wrong and I tried
to fight.

Twinkle, twinkle, little
heart,
Oh, you have been torn
apart.
Deep down in myself so
deep,
Like a jewel, so hard to
keep.

The plane has begun to
dip and roll,
The rubber band
wound too tight,
Falling in the dark with
no light.

What am I going to do?
I've lost my robes of
blue.
They're all covered in
red.
I should like to be
dead.

Just don't let them ever
turn gray,
Cause I'll be no more,
only evil, that day.

Oh, my, is it too late?
Is this really our fate?

Now I lay me down to
sleep,
From my true heart, will
I keep?
And will I never again
wake?
Will my heart always be
to take?

The world, oh, it is end-
ing
Before it had a chance
for beginning.

The end is here.
Is it now?
The end is here.
Is it now?
The end is here.
Yes, the end is here.
Right now.

Snap, it's gone.
The rubber band just
broke.

Somewhere Between the Night and the Rain

Somewhere out there
rain falls upon
the roof of the world
making sounds that en-
hance
the senses.

The smell of rain chokes
me
like some type of poi-
son
threatening to close my
lungs
and drown me it its
sweetness.

The darkness comes
inviting and loving
caressing my skin like a
velvet
wrap that belongs to my
lover
and chills me to the
core.

Lightning streaks across
a black sky
bringing with it double
images

of light on dark
and then the dark on
light
burned into my eyes.

Random are the pat-
terns above
random are the patterns
below
and there is no pattern
then.

Lightning   crashes
through my mind
interrupting thoughts
that should not be
that there are no answers
to
and there never will be.

Perceive the heat of pas-
sion
like the smell of ozone
penetrating the senses.
Then comes the dark-
ness
to chill away the heat
and to sooth the min-
gled desires.

Between.
 sent between.

forever between.□

Rain falls.
lightning crashes.
darkness wraps its lov-
ing arms about me.

Flesh is weak.
depend on the spirit.
shattered it like the
lightning across the sky
end the whole thing like
such a storm.

See stars.
the clouds come like en-
emies in the night.
bringing the rain and
the lightning.
the passion is on the
wind.
I smell it.
I feel it to my core.
the anticipation
like the smell of rain
choking my lungs
in its delicious sweet-
ness
like the smell of ozone
crackling in the dark
in its tantalizing sting

Take me away.
between.
between is where I am.
take me.
somewhere

between the night and
the rain
between.

roses of red

Fire of the windswept
it comes too hot, too
hard
cut my heart with ra-
zors
and tell me
where has it has all gone
to?

Hot and dry
like the windy vice
and in it red
roses fall
petals strewn
to the wind
distributed among
those who don't care
and those who do
cannot catch a
flower petal
that they may live
instead of fading
into the winds
and then the sands
of the hourglass

Over and over
the view catches my eye
the view that cannot be
touched and
oh how

I yearn to
touch the fire
but it will
burn and bring me
to life
which is
more than I am
and less than I was
but it is my desire and
my blood
pattering like rain
upon the asphalt
of the end of time.

Now I see
bloody roses upon my
pillow
greet a too willing
frame.
coldness eternal
seeps
like withered flowers
in a press
like pain
like pleasure
the scent of blood...
or is it flowers...
is strong and will cut my
senses
like rain upon my paper
life.

Images Burning

White hot sounds
blister across my tender
ears.
they make visual memo-
ries
like so much star fire.

Burn inside out
and remind me that I
am
alive.

Or at least at one time I
was.
touch the core and feel
blissful - wonderful - ec-
stasy
pain.

Explain the sweet and
salty
tears like ice dripping
from
oceans of eternity.

Blue blushes feather
gently
across   tepid   green
cheeks
as tender as merciless
torture

that breaks across my
tongue.

Bleeding flowers blos-
som in my sight
dripping aromatic ichor
on my jasper eyes
as in my retina a reversed
image lives
colors oppose and then
they burn.

A fire lit.
burning blue and black
the nighttime stars
are my only witnesses.

Moonlit Meeting

She is here.
He can feel her pres-
ence.
And soon, he can see a
gleam of white.
It is the smooth cream of
her flesh
in the moonlight.
He sees the glistening of
greens,
all colors of greens,
shining under the stars.
Her hair is floating all
around
her sleek body.
It is like a circle of fire
in the sea as he watches.
She stares up at him
with eyes that are
blue-green,
just like the depths of
the sea.
She smiles up at him,
her teeth like pearls
behind ribbons of
coral.
He is breathless.
She dives into the
waves.
There is a glimpse of a
tail of green.

And she is gone.
Was   she   ever   really
there?

Lean

Lean into the wind
find the spot
where the wind finds
your features and blurs
them to infinity and be-
yond.
The rain chills
to the bone-like
fetid breath of morbidi-
ty
stepping on fields of
flowers
blackening by the
touch
of fate and entropy
where they all step.
Runnels of rain water
wash away the tears
of some formation
from the lakes of blue
that were clear
but are now clouded by
the entirety
of life
or the lack thereof
or is it more?
the wind brings the
words
of the end of time
but I can't
understand...

The Note True

Ice trickles in
from all the places deep
and shatters
when the note rings
true.

[why can I not hear the
truth]

Frozen crimson in
hardened veins of blue
pumping through
a heart gone sluggish
with such a crashing
ring.

[find me the truth]

Truth broken apart
like so much crystal ice
scattering shards
to the four winds in a
tinkling   array   of
sound.

[tell me the truth]

I was blind but now I
see
through glasses of clari-
ty

that reveal all that was
hidden
behind a velvet black
veil.

[there is no truth]

Play the note true.
Shatter this reality.

Petals of Blue

Petals, pretty, pretty
petals
from a pretty, pretty
rose,
all nice and blue.

Take the rose
strip the petals
crush the leaves.

Petals, petals, falling
around me
filling up the room.
Blue and thick,
sweet smelling and
blue

Petals, too many rose
petals
they will bury me in
their sweetness.

Falling all around and
I am drowning
In petals so soft and
blue
like water
they strangle me.

Reason of the Ending

To get to the end
start at the end
and go forward
as you go back.
When you lose your-
self
so completely
that you no longer
recognize yourself
you have found the rea-
son
for the end.

I Looked Away

I sat upon the top
and looked...

I sat upon the top
and looked down
into whispered inten-
tions
that have fallen away
from too solid hands.

I sat upon the top
and looked out
into shuttered doubts
that have closed up
from   too   solid
thoughts.

I sat upon the top
and looked up
into veiled memories
that have disappeared
from too solid hearts.

I sat upon the top
and looked in
into mistaken mean-
ings
that have dived down
from too solid souls.

I fell from the top

and looked away...

Fate's Door

The key to faith's door
opens up my fate.
The end of the world is
coming to me.
I sit here and quietly
watch and wait.

It seems to me that the
winds of time are late
because before now this
I could not see.
The key to faith's door
opens up my fate.

Upon my heart, a thirst I
could not sate,
and so it was fate that
this was to be.
I sit here and quietly
watch and wait.

Beyond it all, beyond
this mortal state,
is something to be
opened by this key.
The key to faith's door
opens up my fate.

I shall go alone, for there
is no mate
in this place of quiet, on

bended knee.
I sit here and quietly
watch and wait.

The key to faith's door
opens up my fate.

Trenton Bridge

I walk alone,
And it is dark.
The great bridge is
gone,
sank beneath the sea,
and as it sank,
I sang.

Trenton Bridge is falling
down,
Falling down, Falling
down,
Trenton Bridge is falling
down,
My world has died.

I was on the bridge,
as it sank beneath the
sea,
the deep dark sea,
So I now walk alone,
across a dead bridge
on the bottom of the
sea,
so dark and still, like
death.

I feel Trenton Bridge
Under my plodding
feet,
and I feel the water

all around me.

I walk alone
and it is dark.
Dead and walking a
dead thing,
Trenton Bridge is
naught
but for me.

War Above Sleep

Sleep, child, sleep,
do not wake now,
too much is happen-
ing,
so sleep, dear child,
sleep.

War is raging outside the
door.
You cannot understand
yet.
Your mother sits alone
weeping because she
does not know
if your father yet lives
and fights the masses.

Men die down twenty
feet above you
and you do not know.
Sleep, dear one, don't
think,
for in a year, you may
not sleep like this
any more.
You may be sleeping
forevermore by then.

The Watch

The dragon's eyes are
red in color.
Red as burning coals.
They look upon me.

I work along,
without a thought.
I go along,
unknowing of fate.

Destiny's child,
if you will,
was born today...

And the dragon watch-
es.

Silver and Gold

Silver wind, gold rays of
light
Illumination through-
out.
Coins of silver and
gold,
fallen from a leaden
hand
tinkering like chimes.
Silver mist, gold dew,
weighing down the
world,
so it is not blown away.

The Castle Crumbles

A castle of fragile crystal
and glass
sits upon the hills of
mine own heart,
ripe for the plunder that
is yet to come
from the world that
strives to bring me
down.

A trio of sound finds its
way to me in the night.
A telephone rings like
shattering ice to freeze
my heart.
A million yelling voic-
es break my sanity from
the other end.
A soft whisper then
sends my word into the
oblivion.

I stand frozen and alone,
my being folded in
twain,
like some well-mean-
ing but cheap friendship
card,
but still, here they come
now with their end-
ings,

climbing the steep hills
in mine own heart.

It all comes crashing
down by their blows,
crystal broken down
from glass to sand.
As I watch, the rotten
fruits of my beliefs
have left me naked and
shivering in the night.

Starfire

Suspended shades
ink out the light
and I lose sight
as though blinded
by something
that does not exist

Touch
touch the
touch the stars

I see the silver shadows
silent and venerable
hidden for so long
breaking their bond
cracking the black
with velveteen fingers
splayed
across eternity

Feel
feel the
feel the truth

A burst of light
and   the   cold   world
burns
and I watch silent
as the blinding light
comes to wash
over me

Rosies and Posies

Ring around the
Rosies,
Pocket full of Posies,
Ashes, Ashes,
We all fall down.

Eyes closed to pain.
Ears closed to screams.
Nose closed to rot.
Mouth closed to
mourn.
Hands closed to sense.
But the voices remain.

Death within the
Rosies,
Mourning flowers
Posies,
Ashes, Ashes,
We'll all die down.

I quit seeing.
I quit hearing.
I quit smelling.
I quit speaking.
I quit touching.
The voices don't quit.

Withered saddened
Rosies,
From my hands fall

Posies,
Ashes to Ashes,
Now we are dead.

They make me see.
They make me hear.
They make me smell.
They make me speak.
They make me touch.
And they drive me
mad.
I run and I sing...

Up above me Rosies,
Down beside me
Posies,
Ashes to Ashes,
I am one dead.

Sightless Sounds

around the end of time
I saw your soul
and I found it yet bitter
and   salty   from   my
tears.

around the end of time
I heard your spirit
and I found it sour
and   rotten   from   my
touch.

I made the attempt.
The   flower   of   friend-
ship
I passed it to you
and you batted it from
my swollen hands.

I made the attempt.
The heart of my soul
I showed to you
and you beat it down
with angry fists.

Sounds blur before my
eyes.
Sights scream before my
ears.

So much for what might

have been...

A New World

The time of thunder is
coming.
And the lightning will
precede.
But before all,
the endless rain will be-
gin to fall.

The fantasy, the fairy
tale,
shall become the reali-
ty.
The reality, the truth,
shall become the fanta-
sy.

All life shall be de-
stroyed
only to be reborn
into new shapes that are
unreal now.

Does anyone see the
lightning?
Does anyone hear the
thunder?
Prepare to die.
Prepare to live.

Death and life,
all the same,

from now on.
The rain is falling heavy
now,
and fires are burning,
and the lightning has
come,
and the fire consumes
all,
fed by water instead of
air.

Things are not in con-
junction.
The   thunder   will
come,
and with one resound-
ing boom,
consume all.

All to be reborn
with the first ray of
light
as something new and
mysterious.

Oh, how loud it is!
Resonating forever and
ever and ever and...
All is quiet.

I open my new eyes in a
new world.
The fire is gone.
The rain is gone.
Light surrounds me.

I smile as best I can
and raise golden red
wings,
born from the ashes,
I rise.

Once a myth,
now so true.
I sore over the lands,
mythic lands of lore.

Someone watching be-
low sees
a lone Phoenix in flight.

Lovely to See

Touch me not.
Away, away, away,
and come back.
Don't touch me,
but sit by me.
Stay with me
and do not touch.
Lovely to look at,
Lovely to hold,
but break me,
and I am sold.
No, no, come near
but hands off.
Be by my side
but not too close.
Sold away.
Sold to the dark.
Don't break me.
Don't touch me.

EPILOGUE
Shadow Reflections

The Shadow Dancer stops. Her eyes are closed; her dance is finished.

She breathes, or at least, she appears to breathe. She is no more alive than the dust piled deep in the corners of the disused studio. She senses outside here what is happening, as she always has. But all these years, never has her dance stopped. Day, night, and in between, she would dance on, despite any goings on here and there outside her small studio. Sometimes she wandered, but mostly she danced before the mirror.

This Shadow Dancer, though, has had something happen for the first time in a very, very long time since she was left alone in her little studio. Some days after she had danced, she would go up the stairs and sit upon the bed in a little girl's room that she used to sleep in. Across the hall was a little baby boy's room where her sweet baby brother had once played. And right above the studio had been her mama's room. Some days then, she would go to the room behind the tiny studio storefront, where the dilapidated sofa sat, and near the small and rusting kitchen.

in these many years, the door opened.

The little girl started, hearing the door. It was loud, and there was a sucking sound, like air rushing into someplace that had no air before. The nice young man who had helped them yesterday stayed the night in the abandoned building to ensure they were safe. Her mother lay curled with her baby brother covered by the blanket the young soldier had found for them. She stood up and stared as she saw something from the corner of her eye move around the front of the building.

She followed the movement and found herself staring at a young girl, maybe about fifteen years old, in a pink and purple ballet tutu. She had long black hair that, if not tied up in a high ponytail, might have reached the back of her knees. There was an unnatural silence around them. The girl in the tutu motioned for her to come forward, and the girl did so. She pointed to the now-open doorway that led into the dance studio. The little girl followed her inside.

The dark-haired girl showed her to a locked box that sat high on a shelf and smiled. She took a chain from around her neck and placed it on the little girl. On the chain was a silver key. When the little girl looked up, the girl in the tutu was gone. She went out the door and heard her mother call. She quickly told her mother that a girl had given her this key, took them inside, and showed them the box.

They wondered at the open door and even more at the inside of the small dance studio. It was dirty and dusty but in wonderful condition. The dance bar was still intact, and no rust or ruin was to be found. The young veteran and the young widow opened the small lockbox to find the deed to the building, signed by the owners. There was also a bank account and all the numbers to it. Other than that, there was only a note.

The music has ended for us. Our daughter has succumbed to her illness, as has our baby boy. We are alone in this studio and home, and we know it will no longer be for us. My sweet dancer has left us, and now we leave this place for somewhere else. I have left the key to this lockbox in my lovely dancer's grave around her neck, so unless she wills it, no one will dance in the studio she loved so much.

They looked up in time to see the reflection of a shadowy figure dancing beside them. They turned but found no one there, and when they looked back, nothing but the room they stood in was reflected in the mirror. But the little girl knew better. She took the young man's and her mother's hands, placed them together, then went to the mirror and began to dance before it.

-
-

- https://autismwomensnetwork.org/

Identity First Autistic

- identityfirstautistic@gmail.com

- https://www.identityfirstautistic.org

Mental Health and Mental Health Resources

National Alliance on Mental Health

- 1-800-950-6264

- http://www.nami.org/

Depression and Bipolar Support Alliance

- 1-800-826-3632

- http://www.dbsalliance.org/

National Mental Health Association

- 800-969-6642

-

Trauma/PTSD/Anxiety

Anxiety Disorders of America

- 301-231-8368

National Center for PTSD

- 802-296-5232

- https://www.ncptsd.org

National Victim Center Infolink

- 800-FYI-CALL

Eating Disorder Resources

National Eating Disorders Association

- 800-931-2237 (M-F, 11:30 am-7:30 pm EST)

- http://www.nationaleatingdisorders.org/

ANAD: National Association of Anorexia Nervosa and Associated Disorders

- 630-577-1330 (M-F,12 pm-8 pm EST)

- http://www.anad.org/

Substance Use Disorder/Addiction Assistance

Substance Abuse and Mental Health Services Administration

- 1-877-SAMHSA-7

- https://www.samhsa.gov/

AL Anon Family Groups

- 800-344-2666

- 800-356-9996

- https://alanon.org/

American Council for Drug Education

- 800-488-DRUG

- https://www.acde.org

American Council on Alcoholism

- 800-527-5344

- https://assistedrecovery.com

Harm Reduction Coalition

- 212-213-6376

- https://harmreduction.org

National Institute on Drug Abuse (NIDA)

- https://www.nid.nih.gov

Anonymous Groups

Alcoholics Anonymous

- 212-870-3400

- https://www.aa.org

Cocaine Anonymous

- 310-559-5833

- https://www.ca.org

Co-Dependence Anonymous

- 602-277-7991

- https://www.coda.org

Families Anonymous

- 800-736-9805

- https://www.familiesanonymous.org

Gamblers Anonymous

- 213-386-8789

- https://gamblersanonymous.org

Narcotics Anonymous

- 818-733-9999

- https://na.org

Sexaholics Anonymous

- 866-424-8777

- https://sa.org

Transgender Assistance and Equality

Transgender Youth Equality Foundation

- 207-478-4087

- http://www.transyouthequality.org/

Trans Student Educational Resources

- TSER@transstudent.org

- http://www.transstudent.org/

Bullying Prevention Assistance

Stopbullying.gov

- https://www.stopbullying.gov/

PACERS National Bullying Prevention Center

- 1-800-537-2237

- http://www.pacer.org/bullying/

Suicide Prevention Hotlines and Help

National Suicide Prevention Hotline

- 1-800-273-8255

- https://suicidepreventionlifeline.org/

Crisis Text Line

- Text "Start" 741-741

- http://www.crisistextline.org/

Trans Lifeline

- US: 1-877-565-8860

- Canada: 1-877-330-6366

- https://www.translifeline.org/

Suicide Prevention Resources

- http://www.sprc.org/

The American Association of Suicidology

- http://www.suicidology.org/

American Foundation of Suicide Prevention

- https://www.afsp.org/

GLBT National Youth Talk

- 1-800-246-7743 (M-F, 4pm-12 am EST/Sat, 12 pm-5

pm EST)

The Trevor Project

- 1-866-488-7386 (24/7)

- Text "Trevor" 1-202-304-1200 (F 4 pm - 8 pm EST)

- http://www.thetrevorproject.org/

Warm Ear Line

- 1-866-WARM EAR (927-6327)

- http://warmline.org/

Self-Injury Assistance

S.A.F.E. Alternatives

- 1-800-DONTCUT

- http://www.selfinjury.com/

Human-Created Disaster Helpline

Disaster Distress Helpline

- 1-800-985-5990

- Text "TalkWithUs" 66746

Sexual Violence and Abuse Resources

National Sexual Violence Resource Center

- 1-877-739-3895

- http://www.nsvrc.org/

RAINN- Rape, Abuse, and Incest National Network

- 1-800-656-4673 (National Sexual Assault Hotline)

- https://www.rainn.org/

Domestic and Intimate Partner Violence Resources

The National Coalition Against Domestic Violence

- 303-839-1852

- http://www.ncadv.org/

The National Domestic Violence Hotline

* 1-800-799-SAFE

* http://www.thehotline.org/

The National Resource Center on Domestic Violence

* 1-800-537-2238

* http://www.nrcdv.org/

Human Trafficking Resources

National Human Trafficking Resource Center

* 1-888-373-7888

* Text BeFree (233733)

Runaway and Child Abuse Resources

National Runaway Safeline

* 1-800-RUNAWAY (786-2929) (24/7)

* http://www.1800runaway.org/

USA National Child Abuse Hotline

- 1-800-422-4453 (24/7)

National Safe Place

- Text SAFE and your current location to the number 69866 (24/7)

- http://nationalsafeplace.org/

did, it was apparent they would stick to something other than the every day. Her first story, written in spiral notebooks, was about a kidnapping. There were endless story ideas featuring fantastic places, monstrous creatures, and forbidden love in her mind even then. There's no surprise that these days, they favor the dark corners of the psyche over the happy and fluffy parts. Enamored with the mind, she studied extensively in psychology and related fields. She spends most of her days dreaming about stories and deciding how to make the unruly characters do as they tell them. As everyone knows, sometimes the characters take off and do what they want, no matter what the author has planned.

Beverly's other hobbies include gaming of all types, including a great love of tabletop, transgender and autism advocacy, and writing fanfiction when she can. Their interest in the BDSM community began as a simple curiosity but has led her to the road to finding a place for herself there as a Domme. She has gone on the journey of self-discovery in the last few years, finally pinning down their identity after nearly thirty years of searching. Coming out as bigender, asexual, panromantic, and polyamorous was one of the hardest things they've ever done, but it gave them the confidence to become themselves even more. An autistic person and an eclectic pagan, Beverly finds themself at odds with a lot of what society calls "normal." They don't mind, though, because they find that they are uniquely queer in every aspect of her life, and she's just fine with that.

Beverly started their writing journey seriously in 2013 when she found their way to fanfiction. She spent several years writing over three million words in various fandoms. In the last few years, they have been drawn to making those stories into original pieces and publishing them for a wider audience. Finding her publishing home helped make that dream a reality, one that they try to help others find.

Visit online: https://www.phoenixreal.net/

phoenixreal.net
Queer Love

Crimson
Hunt
Behind the
Red
Part One
Beverly L. Anderson
J Foster

arrives, seemingly an apology for a bit of bigotry from a shop clerk. No one thinks a dress can cause any harm, so he wears it under the stage lights. Things go awry, though, and Kerry wonders what could possibly be happening. A bounty hunter named Martin swoops in, convinced that he can be of aid in the situation. Along with Martin, there's an intrepid FBI agent named Zak on the trail of a pair of sadistic serial killers who target and manipulate young, attractive, feminine men like Kerry.

Kerry doesn't believe it at first. Can he be targeted by these people? Then, things start happening, and his phone and email is full of messages with horrible images of what these people plan to do to him. He's frightened but staunch in living his life. He is adamant that he won't let them win, no matter what they do to him. Still, as the manipulation and gaslighting continue from afar, he starts to doubt everything he's ever known. He begins to lose purchase on reality but finds that Martin and Zak ground him. He refuses to give in to their sadistic games, but in the end, he begins to wonder if his willpower is enough to keep these people away from him.

***

Stolen Innocence - Doctor's Training Part One

When desperate criminals find an easy target in the autistic neurosurgeon Kieran Sung, the young doctor is soon at the mercy of a local Irish mob boss with perverse desires. Despite suffering at his hands, rescue finds him with relative quickness. Pulled unwillingly into circumstances that bring his world crashing down around him and destroying the carefully laid routines and structure he desires; Kieran must find a new way to live. He discovers comfort in ways he never imagined, within sensations of pressure and binding. Taking the hand of a childhood friend who desires nothing else but to help him, Kieran realizes his heart aches for more in his life. Circumstances bind him to a tattoo artist named Varick Jaeger, an actor named Carmine DeAngelo, and a bartender named Devan Sullivan. With this unlikely trio, Kieran must learn how to handle the upheaval in a life he sees desperately needs change.

Stolen Innocence, part one of the Doctor's Training Trilogy, is a story of healing that examines D/s culture, the complexities of polyamory, and how people often deal with mental and physical trauma. Follow Kieran, Devan, Varick, Carmine, and the rest of their pack; they navigate a world that rarely accepts people who do not fit in with expectations.

***

Escaping Fate, Embracing Destiny

CJ Kim is a normal college student. He is doing what most college students do, figuring himself out, sometimes the hard way. He has some strange dreams now and then, but he just thinks they are just dreams. They're certainly nothing to worry about when reality is pressing down so hard on him. Between the demands of school and family, he has enough on his mind.

He ends up with a huge crush on a senior that is on the baseball team. He doesn't even like baseball, but he goes to games just to see him. Of course, he'll never notice a gay and nerdy English major like CJ. Things are good, though. He even has a good relationship with his parents and his twin sisters.

He never expects his family's past to come back to haunt him. It rears its head in the worst way possible and CJ finds himself the prisoner of a vengeful man. Thrust into something that goes beyond what can be considered normal, CJ finds out that there's a fate out there trying to destroy him. He doesn't know how, but he has to reach for a destiny that he can just barely see.

***

Dark and the Sword – Legacy of the Phoenix

Book One

The world of Avern has moved on. It has been almost a thousand years since the day the entire pantheon disappeared. Since the Abandonment, the mortals have learned to live without gods and goddesses. The world became mundane, with little magic and even less hope. Tyrants have risen, and those able to wield what is left of magic are powerful. Forces surge in the darkness that threaten to topple the already fragile world. However, the plight of the world of Avern is not unknown, and those who watch from a distance have decided to intervene. The mortals are sleeping, however, unknowing that two great powers will soon be vying for control.

Then something happens that changes things. A young princess makes a bid for power by murdering her father. She then attempts to murder her sister, the crown princess of Lineria, Keiara. Despite a true strike aided by dark powers, Keiara doesn't die. Instead, the strike pierces the barrier between her human soul and the soul sleeping within her, the soul of the Dark Phoenix. More than a goddess, the Dark Phoenix is the legendary mother of the gods. She is a part of the Eternal Phoenix that brought life to their world eons ago, one of the primal forces of the cosmos.

***

Chasing the Silver Dragon – Part One Disconnect, Book One of the Dragon Trinity Cycle

Silver Dragon has become a bane to the werewolf community in recent years. Designer heroin, one that actually affects were creatures where normal drugs are simply a passing fancy, has infiltrated the St. Louis werewolves. One of these, a young woman named Anna Maddox, wants her brother back somehow from the brink he's standing at. To do this, she reaches out to the ancient order, the Children of Asclepius. Duncan Powell hears her plea and pledges to help her rescue her brother from the streets of St Louis.

He goes to Detective Sebastian Pearce, a member of Unit Zero, the law enforcement agency that deals with supernatural creatures that pose a threat to the peace in the world. Sebastian implores him to leave things to Unit Zero, but Duncan is stubborn and goes down to the Red District to find the young Were. Sebastian and his partner follow and then begin the mission that will either save Kacey Maddox or doom all of them.

***

Let Sparks Fly – Short Story Compilation

Romance can come from the most unexpected places. Sometimes, two people meet, and the sparks just fly between them. Then, sometimes, two people see each other every day, and don't realize the spark that exists between them.

In this volume, you will find stories of many kinds. You'll meet a pair of fellows just looking for a sub to share when they ask out two people, and a secret is revealed. A young man is pining for his very best (straight) friend when a strange entity shows him pleasures beyond imagining, along with some truth. Join a guy who secretly harbors a taboo wish he thinks will never come true. Watch the sparks as a pair of swimming rivals find themselves in a compromising position. A demon on a mountain demands a sacrifice and receives something he isn't expecting. And finally, a man finds his bliss in a woman who can completely own him.

Journey through these pages and enjoy short erotic stories of love found in some quite unusual ways.

***

Whispered Shadows – A Poetry Anthology

The twisting paths of a poet's mind lead to intriguing places, there can be little doubt of this. These places contain whispers of the writer's soul. Some paths show desired sights; others uncover unforeseen knowledge and, at times, unwanted things. The shadows conceal unknown discoveries on well-lit paths through the poet's mind. Travelers, beware: uncertain destinations await along these paths. Tread carefully. Becoming lost in the pages of the poet's thoughts may be a very real danger to these travelers.

So, come along and visit this place of shadows. Here, there be dragons, monsters, truth, and more to enjoy. Fantasy, Reality, and Truths form one hundred and fifty poems by Beverly L. Anderson. The first path is one of fantasy with mythic beasts of yore and darkness that creeps into the very bone. Fairies may fly, and dragons may soar. The second path is one of reality and perhaps questions of what is and is not within that reality. Questions of existence and what the world shows us daily are spoken here. And the final path is one of truths. These truths may be surprisingly uncomfortable or may not be the truth expected. In any case, travel the paths at your own risk.

Open these pages and see if something draws you into the whispered shadows of the very soul.

***

Reflections of the Shadow Dancer

In an abandoned dance studio, there's music and dancing unheard and unseen by anyone. The whispers in the shadows laud praises upon the figure who spins around the room, her body translucent and flickering in the night. Nothing is in motion, and yet everything moves around the room. Darkness and light intertwine and dance to cast the shadows of the world. The Shadow Dancer performs a dance that crosses the borders between the world and other surprising places within flickering shadows.

The Shadow Dancer knows the truth. Without the darkness, there can be no light. Without the light, there can be no darkness. Between them lies the shadow in which the Shadow Dancer twirls.

Enter the world of the Shadow Dancer and immerse yourself in 150 poems, living in the light, the dark, and the shadow.

Confined by Heaven
Chains of Blood
Book One
Beverly L. Anderson
J. Foster

The day started as any other day would. Bellamy Delacroix was shopping with his brother, and then he headed home to the inevitable discussion about his future with his mother. A woman who still cooks despite technology that doesn't require her to, his mother is an old-fashioned type in a future world.

Then, his world explodes quite literally, and he's swept up into a world beyond his imagination. A war between extraplanar creatures who call themselves angels and demons draws him in because of what he is. And what he is, no one has ever seen before—a Nephilim. He is the child of an angelic mother and a demonic father and is thus capable of channeling both the positive and negative energies of the planes. This makes him dangerous and a target for both the minions of heaven and hell.

An angel named Saniel takes him under her wing and helps him adjust as he is brought to the underground city of heaven, Elysium. He learns about what he is, who they are, and their enemies in Zion, the demons. A warning from an ally of his mother, though, rings in his head, and he wonders who he should really be trusting. Things begin to spiral in ways he doesn't understand, and the world is changing before his very eyes.

Released by Hell – Chains of Blood Book Two

Driven insane by the very people he trusted, Bellamy is caught between worlds in a way like never before. He's in the hands of Addariel, the angel both at fault for his fall from grace and the current King of Hell. His mind is only clear when he is inside his own head and his world is spinning out of control. A terrible experiment that went wrong has left him on the verge of death, and it is up to the Codex of Hell and Addariel to save him.

Then, the strangest things happen among the demons. They devote themselves to his salvation, claiming him as their mate and, more than that, dedicating the hearts they didn't know they had to him. In his madness, he captures their very souls and changes the nature of the beasts around him. Even Addariel, once only interested in power, shifts his focus to taking care of the mentally fragile Bellamy. For the first time in Zion's history, the King of Hell cares more for something other than power and conquest.

Elysium, though, is not letting go of him easily. In a misguided attempt to help him, they make a move that could destroy the fragile peace between Zion and Elysium.

Transcended by Earth – Chains of Blood Book Three

Rescuing Bellamy has become a priority for both Elysium and Zion. Adding to the mix are the Arcadians, who will stand to fight for Bellamy. Held by the angel Usiel in a location no one knows, Bellamy fights for his survival and the survival of his unborn child. Usiel wants to breed an army of angels capable of fighting demons without fearing their use of negative energy, and by doing that, he needs to rid Bellamy of the demon's child within him.

A human woman senses something off with a strange neighbor and investigates the situation. What she finds shocks her, and she knows what she must do. Taking Bellamy, unstable as he is, she flees, unsure what to do with what she thinks is a young girl pregnant with her a child her captor wishes to kill.

Meanwhile, in Arcadia, angels from Elysium and demons from Zion work together with a pirate radio station to try and find the missing Nephilim. The world is unsure, but they know they must find him before Usiel captures him again.